WHERE WILTSHIRE
MEETS SOMERSET

Cover: The author approaching Westbury White Horse (Walk 3)
Photo courtesy Susie Jones

Above: A wide track leading from Norridge Farm to Chapmanslade (Walk 18)

Overleaf: Setting out from Buckland Dinham (Walk 4)

Where Wiltshire Meets Somerset

*20 Best Walks in the Country around
Bath, Bradford on Avon, Trowbridge,
Westbury, Warminster & Frome*

by Roger Jones

Maps by Karen Pigott

This revised, reset and redesigned
edition published in 2016
Reprinted with minor revisions 2017
First edition published in 1982

EX LIBRIS PRESS
11 Regents Place
Bradford on Avon
Wiltshire   BA15 1ED

www.ex-librisbooks.co.uk

Origination by Ex Libris Press

Printed by TPM
Farrington Gurney, Somerset

ISBN 978-1-906641-55-9

CONTENTS

Introduction

I came from South Devon to live in Bradford on Avon in the summer of 1980. My first walks out of Bradford were along the towpath of the Kennet and Avon Canal towards Avoncliff. Here the River Avon flows through a steep-sided valley which is garlanded with woods and studded with villages built from the stone of the hills on which they stand. The prospect of Bradford from Barton Farm is very striking, particularly in the morning when the risen sun casts its light directly onto the terraces stacked one above the other on the south-east facing slope. The natural stone shines brilliantly, almost magically, as though it were somehow lit from within.

Turleigh is set high in a cleft on the north bank of the Avon and is followed by Avoncliff, set lower in the valley close by the mills which were once active on both banks. Farther down-river come Freshford and Limpley Stoke. These are all pleasant villages yet I remain especially attracted to the point where the Rivers Frome and Avon unite, where the Frome valley from the south widens to meet the Avon from the east. The stone bridge by The Inn at Freshford, the verdant meadows on the flood plain of the two rivers, the wooded eminence of Staples Hill: all combine to present a vision of great charm and tranquillity. At my first visit there I found the prospect up the Frome valley a great lure. Soon afterwards, as I pressed on along the canal towards Dundas Aqueduct, the valley of the Midford Brook appeared equally enticing.

We had moved into a house in the north-east corner of Bradford on Avon. As Woolley Street rises towards Woolley Green, the houses are replaced by fields which slope away to the south-east, across a wide vale in which Trowbridge is situated, and on towards the chalk escarpment of Salisbury Plain. The White Horse is visible from here but no longer in the company of the tall chimney with its the plume of smoke which served the former cement works just below; it was demolished in 2016. Depending on the weather and the position of the sun, the chalk escarpment can appear very dramatic: like a great tidal wave suddenly frozen in its path north-westwards, and always as a most prominent feature in the landscape.

The hillside upon which much of old Bradford stands is composed of the creamy yellow limestone of which the Cotswold Hills and its towns and villages are made. A cursory examination of a geological map of the area assured me that, geologically speaking at least, Bradford on Avon stands on the slope of a hill that forms the south-eastern edge of the Cotswold range. It is interesting to note that the topographical writer, H. J. Massingham, in his book *Cotswold Country* (Batsford, 1937), deals with the limestone belt which outcrops in ten counties between Dorset and Lincolnshire. Massingham recognised the diversity yet underlying unity of that limestone belt, or 'Cotswold Country', in terms of geology, landscape and building materials.

The western scarp of Salisbury Plain was another feature beckoning me, and so naturally were the towns which lie at its foot, namely Trowbridge, Westbury and Warminster. The Somerset/ Wiltshire border runs more or less north-south a few miles to the west of this string of towns, and even nearer to Bradford on Avon. I followed the valleys of the River Frome and the Midford Brook as they cross the county boundary into Somerset and I am quite convinced that the countryside changes in doing so. On the Somerset side the country seems more broken, more closely divided into hill and vale, somehow more intimate and more like the South Devon with which I was familiar. The Wiltshire side seems characterised more by open spaces, whether upland or lowland.

Cley Hill is an outpost of the Wiltshire chalk just north of the Longleat estate from which one can see Warminster to the east and Frome in Somerset to the west, or north-west and, beyond it, the Mendips. It seemed natural that l should extend my wanderings to Frome and its surroundings. After an initial visit to the town I was hooked. It has a charm and attractiveness totally different to that of Bradford or the other towns of West Wiltshire. Until the removal of the livestock market to an out-of-town site in 1990, it had been a town unique among them. It was as important a centre of the wool and clothing trades as Bradford and Trowbridge, and has the fascinating Trinity area of artisans' houses built in the seventeenth and eighteenth centuries. These dwellings were far removed from the drab rows of identical dwellings which were the norm during the industrial revolution of a later era.

It was during this time that the clothing industry, which was the staple of Frome's prosperity, was lost to the new centres of production in the north of England. This means that, like Bradford, Frome was never much affected by Victorian expansion and redevelopment and both towns maintain the appearance and atmosphere of an earlier time. Frome may lack the architectural riches of Bradford but has instead all manner of interesting backwaters, as befits an old market town.

In the triangle between Frome, Bath and Bradford on Avon there lies a relatively sparsely populated hinterland which is largely dependent on agriculture but which harbours such interesting and attractive villages as Lullington, Wellow and Norton St Philip, all of which are well worth exploring.

In the area dealt with in this book, we find a diversity of landscape represented by the borders of the Mendips, the Cotswolds and Salisbury Plain, three geologically distinct upland areas. The River Avon rises in the Cotswolds and initially follows the dip of those hills in an easterly direction. Unlike her sister streams, which continue eastwards to join the Thames, the Avon flows south through Malmesbury Vale, via Chippenham and Melksham, and then cuts westward through the limestone strata of the 'geological Cotswolds' on its way to the Bristol Channel.

The River Biss, which springs up below the porous chalk strata of Salisbury Plain and which flows by Westbury and through Trowbridge, meets the Avon just up-river from Bradford. Downstream from Bradford, the Avon is joined by the River Frome which rises in eastern Mendip, and later by the Midford Brook, born of the Cam and Wellow Brooks, both of which flow from the Mendip foothills. These rivers and streams and their respective tributaries constituted an essential basis of the wool and cloth industries which have been such an important factor in the growth of the towns and villages in the area here described.

I had originally intended to consider the whole of the boundary where Somerset meets Wiltshire, extending farther south towards Mere in Wiltshire and Bruton in Somerset. However, the Longleat and Stourhead estates constitute a barrier to ramblers on the Wiltshire side and I felt that to include this extension southwards would expand the scope of the book to an unmanageable degree. Not only that, but there are sufficient variety and sources of interest in the area here defined, coupled with an historic unity represented by six hundred years of the wool and clothing trades to provide a suitable country for exploration.

In this latest and completely revised edition I have removed all the incidental notes from the route directions and grouped them at the end of each walk. I hope this declutters the presentation sufficiently that the notes do not distract from the walk itself. But, before embarking on a particular walk, it may be worth casting an eye over the end notes so that you don't miss something of interest.

Roger Jones
Nowhere Cottage
Bradford on Avon
April 2017

Walking in the Countryside

Walking, I am convinced, is the only way to truly appreciate the countryside. The great advantage of walking as a means of getting about the country is its complete flexibility. By that I mean you can go at the pace you choose and, providing you stick to rights of way, you can stop exactly where and when you wish, in order to examine some building or natural feature which presents itself, or simply to admire the view.

I always look forward to setting out on a country walk, and especially that moment when I step off the concrete highway and on to a grassy track or perhaps a field path. Quite suddenly the din and stink of the traffic fades away and the natural sounds take over – the bird song, the wind in the trees and the sound of one's own footfall. Somehow it is a completely different world.

If we wish to walk, where can we do so? In the area where Wiltshire meets Somerset there are a number of country lanes, green roads, tracks and field paths from which we can gain an inside view of the countryside. The ancient network of footpaths is not as complete as it once was. The reason for this is quite simple. Before the age of motor transport, those who lived and worked on farms and in villages had usually to walk to get anywhere. Not that people went very far. Perhaps to the village church on a Sunday or to the nearest market town once a week to sell their produce.

A cursory glance at any large-scale Ordnance Survey map will reveal that the majority of footpaths and minor tracks provide shortcuts from farm to main road, from road to village. Pedestrians always found the shortest route to suit their, as a rule, very local orbit, and it was natural that they should ignore lanes and roads when there was a shorter route across fields or beside hedgerows. Many of these old ways became increasingly neglected in the period after the First World War when motor transport became more widespread. This tendency was even more marked in the twenty or thirty years after World War II. Former rights of way across agricultural land have sometimes been ploughed up and lost without trace, others that have been considered inconvenient or otherwise undesirable by farmers and landowners have been rendered inaccessible by some means or other. In the past I have encountered public footpath notices which have been broken down, tracks between double hedgebanks which have had trees felled across them or mountains of rubbish dumped along their course. There are, too, problems presented in deciphering OS maps which have been rendered obsolete when farmers bulldoze hedges to enlarge fields, or pipe streams underground to improve land drainage.

Yet one can understand the farmer's point of view. Gone are the days when he and his workers used the field paths; now that they no longer have any practical use for country folk, asks the farmer, why should ignorant townsfolk come and trample his crops. I have more than once been engaged in such a discussion with farmers after they had informed me that a public footpath no longer exists across their land and have been sent back the way I came. Yet what remains of our system of footpaths is surely worth protecting. Some town and parish councils and local branches of the Ramblers undertake the task of regularly walking all the rights of way in their areas so that local landowners cannot apply for their closure. There can surely be no objection to people using these footpaths providing they do so with respect and observe the Country Code by closing gates and avoiding all risk of fire. In the long term, the farming community must stand to gain from an increased public awareness of the value of the countryside. It is a precious heritage which belongs to us all; it provides food for the spirit as well as the body.

Having walked all the routes in preparation for this new edition of *Where Wiltshire Meets Somerset* during 2015, it has been encouraging to see what good condition all the rights of way are in, and how well signposted the routes are. There is no doubt that the situation has improved enormously since I first researched this book in the early 1980s. Rambling is hugely popular today, and local authorities have woken up to the fact that the local network of footpaths is an invaluable resource and that their maintenance is a good investment for the tourist industry.

Field crossings, in particular, are generally intact and more efficient than was the case thirty-odd years ago. Signposted step stiles and, more commonly, galvanised steel kissing gates, are most frequently encountered. Such standardised kissing gates may lack the romance of older structures, which perhaps were fashioned courtesy of the local mason, carpenter or blacksmith, but they are built to endure.

A fairly substantial network of footpaths exists near the centres of population, for example around Frome and Bradford on Avon, and in the places generally recognised as beauty spots such as Vallis Vale and the Limpley Stoke valley. There are other areas, relatively far from towns and with unspectacular scenery, such as the hinterland around Norton St Philip, where there are many miles of lanes and minor roads along which little traffic is encountered and which provide suitable routes for walkers.

There are times when it is not easy to keep strictly to public rights of way, particularly when paths cross open fields which have been ploughed or which are packed tight with a standing crop, sometimes over head-height, as is often the case with maize. In such cases it is advisable to make a detour around the edge of the field in order to avoid trampling down crops or negotiating the ridge and furrow of a freshly ploughed field.

Perhaps like you, I am not one to go for a country ramble equipped as though planning to climb Everest. Nevertheless, it should be remembered that, even in the driest weather, you are likely to encounter some mud and that, following a wet spell, it is as well to wear waterproof boots or even Wellingtons. Beware, too, of footpaths in the summer overgrown with brambles and stinging nettles – you will suffer greatly if you wear shorts!

Each of the 20 walks described in this book is accompanied by an appropriate sketch map to show the route taken and the main features to be seen. The maps, together with the detailed description, should be sufficient to guide the rambler. However, anyone with a serious interest is recommended to acquire the relevant Ordnance Survey maps. The two sets of four maps listed below include the routes of all the walks in this book. The Explorer maps are twice the scale of the Landrangers. They are therefore more detailed; in particular, all field boundaries are indicated so they are certainly the more useful for off-road walking.

Explorer Series 1:25,000

(All public rights of way shown in green):
Sheet 155: Bristol and Bath
Sheet 156: Chippenham & Bradford on Avon
Sheet 142: Frome & Shepton Mallet
Sheet 143: Warminster & Trowbridge

Landranger Series 1:50,000

(All public rights of way are shown in red):
Sheet 172: Bristol and Bath
Sheet 173: Swindon and Devizes
Sheet 183: Yeovil and Frome
Sheet 184: Salisbury and the Plain

The Walks

Guide to maps

The sketch maps accompanying the rambles described in this book, together with the directions given in the text will, we trust, provide a sufficient guide to the intending walker.

Key to the maps is as follows:

Route along lane, road ════════════

Route along track ▬ ▬ ▬ ▬ ▬

Route along footpath • • • • • • • • • • •

Why are beaten paths never straight? Even when there are no obstacles!

1 AVONCLIFF

via Freshford, Iford and Westwood

Distance:	5 miles
Maps:	Explorer 142, 156
	Landrangers 172, 173
Map reference:	805600
Refreshment en route:	The Cross Guns pub at Avoncliff; The Inn at Freshford; No. 10 Tea Gardens at Avoncliff

THE WALK is a splendid one by the banks of the Rivers Avon and Frome through a peaceful and delicious countryside. The gorge-like valley at Avoncliff opens out downstream where the Avon is joined by the Frome. The valley from Freshford to Iford is open meadow in its lower reaches, but wooded on its sloping sides. The mellow stone of the bridge, manor house and Italianate gardens at Iford contrasts delightfully with the verdure of the valley. There is a steepish hill to negotiate from Iford up to Westwood and from Upper Westwood down again to Avoncliff.

DIRECTIONS

Avoncliff is reached by road from Bradford on Avon or Westwood. From Bradford you take the Belcombe Road which forks left to follow the railway; the road ends at Avoncliff where there is limited parking space by the canal. From Upper Westwood there is a lane which descends steeply to the canal where chargeable car parking may be found on the left.

To begin the walk, make for the footpath which passes beneath the aqueduct, in the same direction as the flow of the river. You pass by **Ancliff Square** to reach a kissing gate and a hedged footpath a little above the river on your right.

You go through a further kissing gate to reach an open meadow - the path

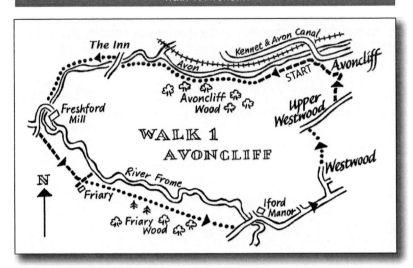

now follows a course close by the river. Carry on until you reach a gate which leads into the hanging woods which here sweep down to the river bank. The woods soon end at a decorative kissing gate where you enter a field – here you follow the beaten path towards a pill box, **Freshford Bridge** and The Inn to the right. The river which flows under Freshford Bridge is the Frome; the Frome joins the Avon just before the railway viaduct down-river.

Cross **Freshford** Bridge and enter a field on the left by a kissing gate to follow a signposted Public Footpath. After about fifty metres the right of way ascends the wooded slope to the right. Follow the path up the hill until you reach a kissing gate. If you bear right here you reach Freshford village – to your right you can see the chimneys and gables of Freshford School. But, to continue the walk bear left, gradually descending the hill again towards the river. The hillside here slopes fairly precipitously and there is an iron fence to protect the walker for the first section.

You finally descend to the level of the river and leave the woods to enter a field by a kissing gate. Carry on in the same direction towards the former mills and through a third gate to reach the lane.

Follow the lane upstream, beside the river, and take the first turning on the left signposted Public Bridleway.

Opposite the main entrance to **Dunkirk Mill** is a fenced track. Follow this until you reach a wood on the right – note views to left towards Staples Hill. Go through a gate and follow the track to a tiny settlement in a cleft reaching down to the valley known as **Friary** (here were sited quarters for the lay brothers from nearby Hinton Priory). Step across the plank bridge, then bear a few yards left before continuing in the same direction. Cross a drive and a field to reach a gate leading into the woods ahead. After a couple of hundred yards the right of way forks left towards a gate and stile to reach a meadow between the hanging wood and the river.

You now bear right to enjoy a clear stretch of field path before reaching the lane at Iford, with hanging woods to the right and the Frome to the left. Bear left to cross the bridge to **IFORD Manor**.

Bear right at Iford Manor up the rather steep hill by the lane towards **WESTWOOD**. You reach the road by the gatehouse to Iford. Bear right and then left into the modern estate known as The Pastures. Bear left at the bottom between the bungalows by a metalled track, then by a path to the left which leads to an old stone stile whose appearance suggests it was here when The Pastures really were the pastures.

Turn right along the lane until you reach Westwood Park and Nursery School on your right. Turn left here by the raised pavement on the right past Westwood Motors.

Follow the pavement until a footpath to the right is signposted along a narrow way between hedges. Follow this onwards and downwards – you encounter various crosstracks but simply keep to the most obvious, direct path until you meet a gate to reach the lane where you carry on and bear left to descend to **AVONCLIFF**.

Gate beyond Avoncliff

BY THE WAY...

Avoncliff is a small but diverse community. There are the remains of two former mills, facing one another on the banks of the Avon; there has been much quarrying and mining of Bath Stone in the hillsides around Avoncliff and, even today, there is a stone mine close by at Upper Westwood. The Kennet and Avon Canal and the railway both pass through Avoncliff, the former crosses the river and railway by a majestic aqueduct and where, since 1906, there is a railway halt. There is a pub, The Cross Guns, with a terrace which looks out onto the aqueduct and weir, and several houses scattered about the river, canal and railway. Access by road, however, is restricted, and only footpaths serve to reach points down-river towards Freshford and up the hill opposite the pub to Turleigh and Winsley.

The mills formed part of the Hungerford Estate in the late fifteenth-century and were used for grinding corn and fulling wool, though they were latterly employed as flock mills, finally closing down at the outbreak of the Second World War. Ancliff Square is a handsome edifice consisting of a continuous group of three-storey buildings facing a courtyard on three sides, all restored during the late 1980s and now

Iford House and bridge

occupied as private dwellings. Ancliff Square was formerly known as The Old Court and was so named during the 1920s when used as a hotel. Before the First World War it housed the Bradford Union Workhouse though its origin predates the Poor Law Act. It was built around 1800; its original purpose is not clear but it is generally accepted that it had some connection with the cloth trade, possibly comprising weavers' workshops and accommodation. There is a domed drying house still standing behind the main building. A detailed and fascinating account of Avoncliff is given in Nick McCamley's book, *Avoncliff* (Ex Libris Press, 2004).

Freshford Mill was originally the property of Hinton Charterhouse Priory and, after the dissolution, fell into the hands of a Trowbridge clothier. It continued as a cloth mill, and latterly as a flock mill, under various owners and tenants, until the Second World War. After the war it was used for the manufacture of rubber products, left derelict for many years but has recently undergone extensive restoration.

The building to the right is Dunkirk Mill which dates from the eighteenth century and, after standing empty since 1912, was converted into a dwelling house in the 1980s.

Iford Manor has an attractive early eighteenth century façade, though parts of the house are much older. The buildings on the left, with the fine oriel window, are the former stables, now converted into a pair of cottages. The gardens, with cloisters and colonnade and many fragments of ancient sculpture collected mainly from Italy, are quite unexpected along this quiet stretch of the River Frome.

Iford Manor is listed in the Domesday Book; it was purchased by Sir Thomas Hungerford in 1369, whose family held it for three centuries. In 1899 Iford was acquired by the architect Harold Peto, who set about creating his unique garden on this favourable south-facing slope. The gardens are regularly open in the summer months, including the Iford Festival, the high point of which is opera. A booklet on the manor and gardens is available. The picturesque Iford Bridge is of medieval origin and is supposed to have been built by the Carthusian monks from Hinton Charterhouse around 1400; Mr Peto erected the figure of Britannia.

2 BECKINGTON

••

via Rode, Woolverton, Laverton and Lullington

Distance:	6 miles
Maps:	Explorers 142, 143
	Landranger 183
Map Reference:	801518
Refreshment en route:	The Red Lion at Woolverton
	The Woolpack Inn at Beckington

Note of caution: It is necessary to cross the busy A36 twice; the first being on a fast stretch of road. There is no danger if you wait for a suitable gap in the flow of traffic though it is always slightly unnerving, especially if you have children with you.

THE WALK passes through five diverse villages. Most of the walking is by field paths although there is a stretch of lane between Woolverton and Laverton, but you are unlikely to encounter much traffic there. An ancient track takes you west from Rode to cross the River Frome by Scutt's Bridge, a former packhorse bridge, unwidened and accessible only on foot, like the bridge at Tellisford a little further down-river (Walk 13).

The cross-country walking between villages will surely convince you that there really is no better way to appreciate a rural landscape than on foot; the route from Woolverton via Laverton, Lullington and back to Beckington has a refreshingly remote feel about it, and is really quite surprising in this respect.

Beckington may be familiar to many who live in the district where Somerset meets Wiltshire as a large village lying close to the junction of two main roads: the A36 Bath-Warminster and the A361 Frome-Trowbridge roads. The bypass, which opened in 1989, has restored Beckington to a peace which almost predates the motor age.

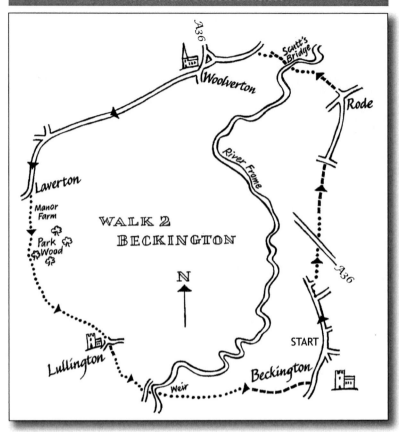

DIRECTIONS

The village main street is wide and you should have no problem parking your car.

To begin the walk: At the northern fringe of Beckington you reach a road junction with the road to Trowbridge to the right. The building ahead is **Beckington Memorial Hall**. At the entrance to the car park look out for a footpath sign indicating the way across the playing field in a diagonal direction and heading for a kissing gate on the far side.

Once through here follow the beaten path towards and beside the hedgerow on your right until you reach a double step stile and the road. At the end of the crash barrier prepare to cross the road. You may have to wait a while for a break in the traffic but you have a good long view in either direction so when you get your chance - go for it!

On the far side drop down just beyond the crash barrier to reach a similar wooden stile. Cross here and follow the hedgerow on the right and keep your eyes peeled for the remains of a kissing gate on your right. (If you begin bearing left to reach the gap at the top of the field you will have gone too far).

Go through this kissing gate to reach a lovely tree-lined path which you follow until you reach a minor junction of lanes. Carry straight on for **RODE**. The River Frome flows unseen in the valley to your left, the tower of Rode Church can be glimpsed across fields to your right.

Exit Crooked Lane and bear right into High Street, then turn left into **The Mead (Merfield Lodge** is the house on the corner). Once past the houses on your right, the road abruptly reverts to a stony, tree-lined track and leads down towards the River Frome. As the way levels out, look out for a kissing gate on your left.

Follow the course of the former mill stream on the right, until you reach a bridge, indicated by a Public Footpath sign, which leads to the three-arched **Scutt's Bridge**, a packhorse bridge across the River Frome.

Cross Scutt's Bridge, follow the fence on the left and continue by the enclosed track ahead. Bear left at the lane and walk on into Woolverton, taking the left fork at the Red Lion. As you reach the main road you will see the little spire of **WOOLVERTON Church** (declared redundant and converted into a private dwelling).

Cross the road, with great care, and very soon turn right along the lane to **Laverton**. Pass a lane joining from the left. Further along you encounter a crosstrack, the northern section of which represents a short piece of the Poole-Bath Roman road; the southern section became the old Henhambridge Way.

When you reach a fork bear left (signposted to Buckland Dinham) descend to **LAVERTON** which has its own immaculately maintained church, St Mary's, but which is little more than a hamlet. Leave the road and walk through the churchyard to the right of the church to reach a gate on the far side of the graveyard. Cross over and enter a farmyard.

Bear left to reach a gate; cross here and turn right, as indicated. Pass through a further gate, cross a track and a stile and continue in the same direction. Now look out for a stile in the hedgerow on your left.

Cross over and bear right. The field narrows where it meets a wood. Cross a stile in the very far corner where you enter the wood, albeit briefly.

Climb up on the left and emerge into a field. Now follow the hedgebank on your right to the field end. Enter the next field and turn left to follow the headland as it twists and turns until you reach a wooden stile. From here you can see the buildings of **LULLINGTON** village. Cross this final field to reach a pair of stiles, then bear right to reach a gate in the field corner, then left along the track beside buildings. Now turn right too reach **All Saints Church** on your right.

Below the church bear left and right past the house called Middle Thatch. Bear right at a traditional red telephone box down a metalled track. Just before the house ahead bear right to cross a stream via a pair of signposted gates and follow the stony path beside the trees to the left. The grounds of Orchardleigh House are to the right, much of which has been converted into a golf course.

Bear left at the end of the line of trees to leave the stony track and follow a beaten path beside the stream which takes you down towards the River Frome. As you cross the metalled driveway, leading to Orchardleigh House to the right, look left for a view of the rather impressive gatehouse known as Gloucester Lodge.

You reach a lane by a stile. Cross the stile opposite, then bear right to cross the footbridge which spans the **River Frome**. Cross the stile on the left and head diagonally across the field, past a pill box to the left, to reach a stile beside a gate. Now bear left.

Carry on beside the field boundary to your left until you reach a stile beside a drive. Cross to the right of way opposite and follow the well defined path beside pheasant enclosures until you reach a drive which soon leads you to **Mill Lane** and the main street through Beckington.

Bear left and continue until you reach the southern end of **BECKINGTON** village.

BY THE WAY...

Beckington: A stroll around the village is well worth the effort and, without the through traffic, is much more enjoyable than before the bypass was opened; the village boasts a wealth of fine stone buildings and an interesting church.

St George's Church stands handsomely in its churchyard, and its most impressive feature – a fine Norman tower – at once captures your attention. Inside, the church contains much of interest. There are several monuments, including one on the west wall to Samuel Daniel, the poet, who died in 1619. There is a piscina, a timbered roof above clerestory windows and several fine corbel heads.

Bear left at the churchyard gate and walk on to Beckington Castle, a three-storeyed, sixteenth-century mansion with three gables facing the street and a castellated porch and stair turret at the side. Bear right here by the former main road (now a cul de sac) and right again at the present road. Opposite is the entrance to Stubbs Lane where the conical roof of a little gazebo marks the boundary wall of Beckington House, a three-gabled house set back from the road. Cross the road and bear left. Just below is a

Street scene, Beckington

most attractive Baptist Chapel dated 1786 and, beyond that, on the same side, a former coaching inn, now a private house, where the iron support of the inn's name board still projects from the wall.

Back on the main road you can see The Grange and Beckington Abbey on the opposite side, parts of which date from the sixteenth-century – these buildings have ecclesiastical origins though details are obscure. Continue through the village, past many old and attractive houses. Beckington is a sizeable village and its many substantial houses bear witness to a former prosperity founded on the wool trade.

Scutt's Bridge Just up-river from this packhorse bridge is a three-arched stone bridge across a mill stream which at this point returns to the river, having been diverted to supply the former Scuttsbridge Mill, now demolished.

Lullington is a most attractive small village with a gem of a Norman church at its centre. All Saints has a splendid northern doorway (see opposite) which can easily be missed if you do not walk right round the church but merely enter by the south door. The plan of the church is unusual in that the tower is at the centre, between the nave and chancel. Inside, the columns at the four corners of the tower are most elaborate and make a fascinating study. The church also contains an inscribed and much decorated Norman font. Lullington village is quiet and well preserved although the school is now a house and there is neither shop nor pub, so almost somnolent.

Faces in stone above the porch at Lullington church

Norman north doorway at All Saints Church, Lullington

3 BRATTON CASTLE

*via Upton Cow Down, Old Dilton, Chalford
and Westbury White Horse*

Distance:	8 miles
Maps:	Explorer 143; Landrangers 183, 184
Map Reference:	899514
Refreshment en route:	The Bell at Chalford on the A350, located just before the last leg of the walk.
Note of caution:	It is necessary to cross the busy A350 twice;

the first being on a fast stretch of road. There is no danger if you
wait for a suitable gap in the flow of traffic though it is always
slightly unnerving, especially if you have children with you.

THE WALK is a longish but exhilarating one. The path from Bratton Castle
along the chalk escarpment is exposed and windswept and the bare downs
afford no protection from the elements. It is advisable to set out on a clear,
sunny day as the views are far and wide. Bratton Castle is an impressive Iron
Age hill fort which encloses a long barrow of the Bronze Age. It is generally
accepted, though unproved, that the Battle of Ethundun, described in the
Anglo-Saxon Chronicle as the battle at which King Alfred defeated the
Danes, took place near here, by the village of Edington which lies under
the scarp to the north-east. Tradition has it that the White Horse was cut to
commemorate the great victory, though others argue that it dates from the
early eighteenth century. The redundant and exceptional St Mary's church
at Old Dilton provides a haven after the stiff walk across open down.

DIRECTIONS

Bratton Castle may be approached from Bratton village or from Westbury.
There is ample car parking in the designated areas under the south-facing
ramparts.

To begin the walk, make for the metalled track which runs along the top of the scarp away from Bratton Castle in a south-westerly direction (towards Westbury). At the quarry entrance, where the road bears right, carry straight on.

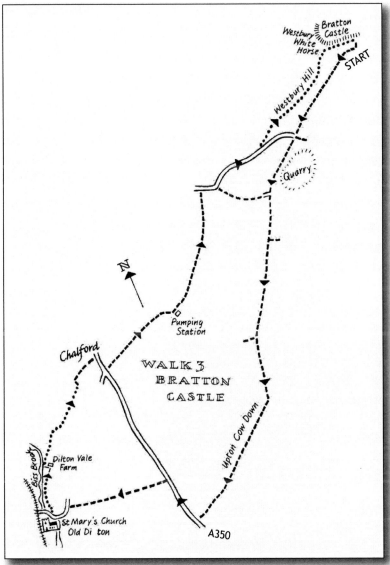

Continue along the high, straight track. Your way now is quite unmistakable. Simply carry on along the stony track, ignoring all footpaths and bridleways signposted to right and left.

This scarp-top track is part of the Imber Range Path, a 30-mile circular route around this western section of Salisbury Plain.

After about a mile the track deviates slightly from its direct course, first left and then right, to negotiate the eminence of **UPTON COW DOWN** whose summit is marked at 199 metres on the Explorer map.

As the path descends <u>keep your eyes peeled for a 6-bar metal gate</u> on the left. Hop onto the bank directly opposite and follow the beaten path which at first runs parallel to the track and then veers to the right. (If you miss this path just carry on until you meet the former main road – note the cat's eyes – and turn sharp right through the gap beside the gate).

This is the former A350. Redundant as a road, this old way now provides a hazard-free means of reaching the next stage of the walk.

You arrive at a point where the old road ends and a Bridleway sign points across the main road. The A350 is always busy so do take care when crossing. Once across you pass through a gate to follow the straight track through fields towards Old Dilton Farm.

Bear left at **Old Dilton Farm** by the lane. You are now descending through Greensand strata and the lane is characteristically sunken. Cross the bridge over the infant Biss Brook (the stream which flows through Trowbridge) to reach **St Mary's Church** in **OLD DILTON** which stands cheek by jowl with the railway bridge and embankment behind.

On leaving the church, turn back over the bridge and look out for a Footpath sign, where you bear sharp left to reach a kissing gate by which you enter a field. Follow the hedge on the left beside the Biss Brook until you reach a further two kissing gates.

After the third gate carry on by the indicated path through the yard of **Dilton Vale Farm**. Turn left and very soon look out for a signposted path on your right. Follow the path before the redbrick house until you reach a footbridge across the brook.

Here you bear right across a tributary stream and by a kissing gate to climb directly up the slope (the Greensand escarpment) by the beaten path, keeping to the right of a pair of trees. At the top pass through a metal kissing gate to follow the hedge on your right. Soon you pass through another gate on your right to follow a fenced path between fields, then beside a fence on your left.

When you reach the cross-track you turn left and then sharp right by the enclosed path, then soon bear right by a path between fields on your right and house gardens on your left. This eventually leads to a short flight of steps which drops you onto a pavement beside the A350.

If you bear left towards the junction a hundred yards or so below you will find the Bell Inn at **CHALFORD**, should you desire refreshment before tackling the final stage of the walk.

Otherwise, with your back to the staircase, turn right and then left to leave the main road by **Wellhead Drove** (left if you are leaving the pub). This lane leads past a few grand houses and beside fields to woods ahead. Take the left fork at the red-brick Westbury Waterworks pumping station.

Past the **Waterworks** the track reverts to a green lane which follows a pleasant course below the scarp whose crest you walked along earlier.

You eventually reach the road which leads from Westbury at the **White Horse Equestrian Centre**. From this point the **WESTBURY WHITE HORSE** is clearly visible and is our target from here onwards.

Turn right at the road and continue climbing for almost half a mile. Look out for a Public Footpath sign beside a kissing gate on the left leading beside fields towards the White Horse and the ramparts of Bratton Castle. Cross the stile here to enjoy the spectacular last stage of the walk (see front cover picture). The right of way follows the edge of the steep escarpment towards the White Horse.

Cross a final kissing gate and leave the cultivated fields to find a toposcope on the crest of the scarp.

Carry on until you reach the ramparts of **BRATTON CASTLE**. From here you should be able to spot your parked vehicle.

BY THE WAY...

Salisbury Plain On leaving leaving Bratton Castle, at the start of the walk, you will see, immediately on your left, the entrance to a former chalk quarry. Here chalk was dug to provide one of the raw materials for the cement works which was situated below the Castle. You can get a good view of the enormous excavation from the track a little further on. The vertical walls of the quarry give an excellent cross-section through the near horizontal chalk strata, distinguished by lines of flint nodules. The quarried chalk was crushed and mixed with clay which was dug from the ground adjacent to the works; the resultant mixture then baked in kilns to make cement.

There are firing ranges within earshot to the left and official warning notices. However, the track ahead is a designated right of way and some distance from the rat-tat-tat of gunfire. Ahead looms the village of Upton Scudamore with the instantly recognisable hump of Cley Hill beyond. As the track descends from a high point near the summit of Upton Cow Down you have a splendid view across a dry valley and into the wild hinterland of Salisbury Plain towards the lost village of Imber, though it is not visible.

Wellhead Drove
The beech wood and dell on your left mark the boundary between the Greensand and the Lower Chalk – the track ahead takes you onto the Lower Chalk which forms a terrace below the chalk scarp.

If you scramble down into the dip directly opposite the Waterworks you will discover the spring, or Wellhead, above the impervious clay of the Gault formation.

Bratton Castle
The height above sea level is 754 feet and, on a clear day, you can spend time finding all the landmarks indicated, and a few more besides. In the fields below, between the scarp and the cement works, if the aliens are about, crop circles may be seen.

The double bank and ditch of the Castle's southern perimeter are well preserved and of impressive proportions. If you still have sufficient energy, it is worth scaling the fortifications to reach the enclosure which contains in its 25 acres a rather mutilated long barrow.

St Mary's Church, Old Dilton

St Mary's Church, Old Dilton

St Mary's was declared redundant in 1973 but is maintained under the Churches Conservation Trust – the church is generally locked but the key is available from a nearby house. The low, perpendicular exterior, with its bell turret and variety of windows, encloses a nave and north aisle and an entirely unspoilt eighteenth century interior; every available space has been utilised for the installation of box pews, some of which incorporate medieval originals and fragments of a former screen.

Unusual kissing gate, partly fashioned from old boiler plate? Near Old Dilton

4 BUCKLAND DINHAM

via Orchardleigh, Spring Gardens and Elliots

Distance:	5 miles
Maps:	Explorer 142
	Landranger 183
Map reference:	755513
Refreshment en route:	There are no opportunities en route but
	there is a pub, The Bell, in Buckland Dinham

THE WALK is fairly easy going through delightful country. There are field paths, tracks through woods, hills with distant views, ancient churches, streams, footbridges and riverside meadows: an unspectacular but nevertheless very appealing slice of rural Somerset.

DIRECTIONS

Facing Buckland Dinham church from the approach road bear right along the signposted Public Footpath. Follow the wall on the right until you reach a gate to enter a field which slopes away towards Buckland Brook.

Walk down across the field to reach a wooden footbridge in the bottom left corner, follow the field boundary and cross a ditch. Cross the next field diagonally via a solitary tree to reach the top left corner – if there is a standing crop it may be advisable to follow the beaten path around the left-hand boundary of this field to reach the same spot.

Leave this field and enter the next by a stile beside a gate on the right. This field is narrow at this end; follow the hedgerow on your left and climb steadily, beside the hedge, until you reach a gap at the top left corner of the field to enter a wood.

Continue in the same direction along a roughly worn track through woods,

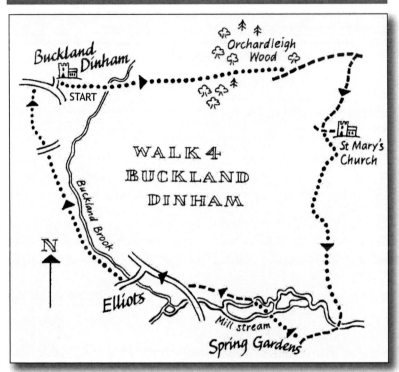

passing buildings away to the right. The main track now soon bears to the left; however, <u>you head straight on</u> to emerge at a clearing. Carry on, bearing left, to reach the drive, gate and cattle grid at the entrance to Orchardleigh golf course.

Follow the drive towards **Orchardleigh** House as far as some buildings on the right until you reach a track joining from the right signposted '**Church**'. Turn right here and follow the track until the belfry of the church comes into view. You pass through a gate and cross a footbridge to reach the little island on which stands the tiny, ancient church of **St Mary**, these days, sadly, generally kept locked and bolted.

Leave the gate by which you entered the churchyard and retrace your steps for 50 metres or so along the track. Bear left up the slope by a fenced track. At a crossing, the track reverts to a footpath, but is still neatly fenced. At the top of the ridge, a gate allows us across a narrow **aircraft runway** to reach the continuation of the fenced path on the far side.

Simply follow the beaten path as it begins its descent on the far side of the ridge to cross a stile into a field. Now carry on in the same direction, crossing three more stiles, keeping the hedge to your left, until you reach a stone bridge across Mells River.

Follow the lane ahead. The restored and converted **SPRING GARDENS Mill** can be seen away to your right.

Look out for the gated entrance on your right; this is the drive to Jeffries Mill. Now look for the stile set in the stone wall, together with a Public Footpath sign, just beyond. Cross the small field here and carry on to cross a drive to enter another field. Continue in the same general direction beside the hedgerow on your left.

Cross a stile beside a gate, then a second stile and a third one to cross a drive. Continue in the same general direction towards the tree-lined stream beyond.

About 20 yards to the left of the sluice gate through which you will hear the rush of water there is a stone footbridge, not always obvious in the undergrowth. Cross this bridge, climb the stile on the far side and head across the field towards another footbridge to the left of the farm buildings. Now bear left along the drive from **Brookover Farm** to the main road which you reach at a point where an entrance gateway to the Orchardleigh estate is flanked by lodges.

Bear right up the main road for a short distance (do take care and walk in single file facing the oncoming traffic). You must cross over at some point and it may be advisable to do so sooner in order to avoid approaching a rather sharp right-hand bend which restricts the view ahead. Turn left down a minor road through the hamlet known as **ELLIOTS**.

Once across the bridge and past the buildings look out for a stone stile beneath a spreading beech tree. Leave the lane here and head down across the field to reach a wooden stile and footbridge opposite.

You now follow a pleasant field path beside **Buckland Brook** towards **BUCKLAND DINHAM**, where the church tower soon hoves into view. There are various field crossings to negotiate; the right of way is visibly beaten all the way – keep the brook on your right and you won't go wrong.

As you enter the final field below the houses make for the gap between the buildings. Here you will drop down onto the lane via a stone slab stile. The field path continues directly opposite. Make for a stile in the top left corner, beside the bench with its commemorative inscription, then follow the hedgerow on the right. Cross two more stiles and a kissing gate before reaching houses. Simply continue in the same direction until you reach the main road where you bear left for The Bell pub and right for the church.

BY THE WAY...

Buckland Dinham is an attractive ridge-top village set on a spur of land about three miles north-west of Frome. It was once a centre for the cloth industry. The church of St Michael and All Angels is found a short distance uphill from the main road which passes through the village. Interesting features include an elaborate perpendicular tower and a doorway and two windows of the Norman period. Inside there is a Norman font, a Lady Chapel on the south side which was restored by the Victorians and a north chapel which contains two effigies – a knight and his lady. These figures represent the donor Sir John Dinham, who died in 1332, and his wife. The original Dinham was Oliver de Dinant who held the manor in 1205 and hailed from Dinan in Brittany. Notice the old blind house just outside the church. (The author once had a ghostly encounter in this church – see page 39).

Left, Lych gate and tower at Buckland Dinham church

Right: Entrace to Orchard-leigh church-yard

St Mary's Church, Orchardleigh

Stroll round the church to view some of the gravestones. Those of the Duckworth family, until recently of Orchardleigh House, are grouped at the far side facing the lake. Just behind them and lying under the yew tree are two small stones inscribed with the name of Henry Newbolt, Poet, and his wife Margaret, née Duckworth.

In his poem, 'Fidele's Grassy Tomb', Newbolt relates the story of the squire of Orchardleigh who, on his death bed, asked for his dog Fidele, who had once saved his life, to be buried at his feet in the family chapel. This was done, but when the Bishop of Bath and Wells heard that a dog had been buried in church he ordered that the parson remove Fidele to the churchyard beside the lake. The sexton was given instructions but could not bring himself to disturb Fidele. In the words of Henry Newbolt:

> *The grave was dug; the mason came*
> *And carved on stone Fidele's name*
> *But the dog that the Sexton laid inside*
> *Was a dog that never had lived or died.*

> *So the Parson was praised, and the scandal stayed,*
> *Till, a long time after, the church decayed,*
> *And, laying the floor anew, they found*
> *In the tomb of the Squire the bones of a hound.*

On the outside wall of the porch is an inscribed plate referring to Fidele's memorial nearby.

The church itself consists only of nave, chancel, bellcote and north chapel. Notable features include the stained glass, priest's door, piscina and aumbry and especially the various carved heads, including two either side of the sanctuary which formerly supported the Lenten veil. The church survived the Reformation fairly intact and was sympathetically restored in 1879; most of the carved heads and much of the stained glass is medieval.

During my last visit, in preparation for this new edition, the church was firmly locked. With its picturesque situation, St Mary's currently attracts a stream of couples using it for their wedding ceremony, but it's a shame this hospitality cannot be extended to the curious rambler.

The Down, Orchardleigh

This is the name given to the ridge (now partly occupied by an airstrip) between valleys – the north dammed to accommodate Orchardleigh Lake; the south along which flows Mells River. From the Down look back for a view of Orchardleigh House and the lake below it. In other directions may be seen the following: to the east the Westbury White Horse, to the south Cley Hill, then the wooded hills of Longleat with the town of Frome in the foreground.

Orchardleigh Church: carved head

A ghostly encounter at Buckland Dinham

The first time I visited the church here I had an odd experience. It was a gloomy Sunday afternoon when I entered. As the door slammed shut behind me and I stepped into the nave I immediately sensed there was someone else in the church. I instinctively looked towards the chancel and saw a figure – a thin, wizened fellow dressed in black and holding a Bible or prayer book. He stood beside the choir stalls and stared at me intently.

He seemed neither hostile nor friendly but looked at me as though I had interrupted him. I was somewhat taken aback and for a moment glanced the other way. When I looked back he was gone and I realised I had seen a ghost (and I am not one given to seeing ghosts!)

I have visited the church since but have not had a repeat experience. My only explanation is that I had disturbed the ghost of some former incumbent carrying out his Christian duties on a Sunday when the Church was empty.

5 CLAVERTON

via *Bushey Norwood, Bathampton Down and Kennet & Avon Canal*

Distance:	6 miles
Maps:	Explorer 155
	Landranger 172
Map Reference:	788642
Refreshments en route:	None, but plenty of places to picnic

THE WALK is a longish but exhilarating one which includes a trek around Bathampton Down with its far-reaching views over Bath and the hills beyond – Lansdown, Little Solsbury Hill, Charmy Down, Banner Down and Bathford Hill. All these hills are essentially composed of near horizontal strata of Oolitic Limestone, or Bath Stone, once much worked in this locality as a source of excellent building stone. Indeed, there are many signs of quarrying to be seen in the perambulation of Bathampton Down, the ascent of which is by lane from Claverton and entails a steady climb over about half a mile; the descent to the Kennet and Avon Canal is considerably steeper. This section can be avoided and the walk shortened by retracing your steps when you return to point A. There are no pubs anywhere on this walk but Bathampton Down provides a choice of picnic sites, so long as you are careful not to obstruct the golf course.

DIRECTIONS

With your back to Claverton church bear right through the village until you reach the lane; here turn right to ascend Bathampton Down. The lane curves first to the left, then to the right; the woods to the right grow within the grounds of Claverton Manor. The valley to the left below forms a steep and narrow cleft in the Down in which Vineyards Farm is situated. You pass the entrance to **Claverton Manor** (the American Museum).

Carry on until you reach a green steel gate on the right bearing a Public Footpath sign. Better to continue a little further until you spot an old stone stile in the form of projecting stone steps set into the wall, signposted Bath Skyline Walk. Cross here and bear right, then left to follow the beaten path beside the fence on your left. Cross another attractive old stile (illustrated on the page 43) to enter National Trust land known as **BUSHEY NORWOOD**.

Take pause here because the route is not obvious. The Public Footpath sign points straight on but this we ignore. Instead bear half left to skirt the copse of trees, then proceed with the copse on your right towards the line of fenced trees in the distance. You may notice a series of upright stones here – the first is in the midst of the copse and there are another two which we walk past along the edge of the trees (see picture page 45).

Once you reach the rough line of cradled trees ahead carry on towards the wooded field boundary, keeping the wooded boundary to your right, until you reach the far corner where you will find a kissing gate. Keep to the main path through the wood, gradually losing height.

You are somewhat below the summit of the down; there is higher ground to the left and the hillside falls away steeply to the right. There is much evidence hereabouts of former quarrying activity in the shape of numerous mounds and hollows.

Simply stick to the most well beaten path. The woods thicken until you reach a cross-path, descending from left to right. There is a **Bath Skyline** sign on the fencepost opposite. Do not cross here but bear left up the old trackway. Soon the path begins to level out. Keep you eyes peeled for an iron stile on your right. (If you reach a sign indicating a way to the left you have gone too far.)

Cross the stile and head straight on through the trees – simply follow the beaten path, through a wooden kissing gate, until you emerge into the open on the slopes of **BATHAMPTON DOWN** which here face towards the north.

You now follow the right of way for some distance with the woods to your right and two masts just to your left. The path joins a track in the vicinity of the masts until it reaches a stile beside a gate. Carry on past the **Bath Golf Club** to reach **Sham Castle**.

To continue the walk: from Sham Castle retrace your steps for a few yards. As you reach the Golf Club's car park turn right by an indicated foopath to follow the track beside the hedgerow, ascending gradually. The track forks as it levels out and reaches a clump of trees to the right. Bear left and cross the fairway of the golf course by a lightly beaten path towards a gap in the line of trees ahead. Pass through the gap and turn left at the signposted embankment ahead.

Follow the embankment traversing Bathampton Down as far as a T-junction marked by a pair of Public Footpath signs indicating Bridleway to Bathampton to the left. Head straight on, beside the fifteenth tee, to reach the edge of a former quarry.

Bear right and follow the boundary fence to its end where you bear left to make a rough and rather steep descent to the base of the quarry. Bear right along the excavated hollow by the beaten path to exit the quarry by squeezing through a gap in the fence. Bear left beside the fence and begin to descend by the steep, direct track which you earlier partly ascended. (If you wish to omit this stage of the walk you can retrace your steps by turning right to reach Bushey Norwood.)

To continue the full route continue to head down this steep track but take care as it can be slippery underfoot in damp conditions. Continue the descent until you reach the main road far below.

As the track approaches the main road it bears left beside houses to reach the road. Cross over with care and turn right. As the bend straightens out look for a public footpath sign on the left - climb over the stile and continue down to Bathampton Swing Bridge and cross the KENNET & AVON CANAL.

Turn right along the towpath and follow it for about a mile and a half towards Claverton. Climb up to cross bridge no. 179. Follow the lane signposted to Claverton. Look out for a stile on the right which affords a short cut to reach the main road via a kissing gate.

Cross the road with care and head for the opening to a path beside the bus shelter opposite. This leads you directly to the main street through CLAVERTON.

Old stone slab stile at entrance to Bushey Norwood

BY THE WAY...

Claverton (the name means the farm where burdock grows) is a linear village on the lower slopes of Bathampton Down arranged along a street which runs parallel to the main road a short distance below. In the centre are some attractive terraces enclosed by stone walls; these are all that remain of the old manor house, which dated from the late sixteenth century. The house was rebuilt in the early eighteenth century much higher up the hill with commanding views across the valley of the River Avon. Claverton Manor now houses the American Museum, so allowing the public access to the house and grounds.

Claverton's St Mary's Church may be reached by a footpath from the village street. The church was heavily restored in the mid-nineteenth century and is unusual in that the chancel appears to be as long as the nave. The church contains a striking monument to Sir William Basset (died 1613) and his wife. This is in the form of brightly painted life-size sculptures of the couple set upright in niches in the side of the chancel. Outside there is a good example of a scratch dial on the porch and, in the churchyard, Ralph Allen's mausoleum crowned with a great stone pyramid. Ralph Allen was a good friend of Richard Graves who was rector here for 55 years. Also in the churchyard are the graves of four of Cromwell's soldiers who were killed in action in 1643, Claverton Manor having been captured by the Parliamentary General, Sir William Waller.

Bridge over the Kennet & Avon Canal

Mere Stones Look out for a series of upright stones at Bushey Norwood – the first may be spotted within the copse and a further two along its edge. The picture below shows the third stone at the far edge of the copse. Bathampton Down was settled and cultivated in pre-Roman times; these are the remnants of mere stones which were set up to mark field boundaries.

Mere stone, Bushey Norwood.
This is the third stone as it is approached, near end of the copse.

Sham Castle, an artificial ruin, was erected in 1762 by Ralph Allen, to beautify the view from his townhouse in North Parade in Bath, Prior Park having not yet been built. It is perhaps surprising that anyone should wish to create an artificial ruin, but perhaps even more surprising that the eighteenth-century love of order should demand that the Sham Castle's façade be absolutely symmetrical. But whoever heard of a symmetrical ruin? The view back to Bath reveals a few familiar landmarks like the Abbey and the Empire Building.

Bathampton Down was certainly the site of a pre-Roman settlement as the tumuli and evidence of Iron Age agriculture testify. It is likely that the embankment is a surviving fragment of a linear earthwork built to protect the original Iron Age enclosure. Some authorities refer to the earthwork as part of the post-Roman Wansdyke and its form – a simple ditch and north-facing bank – and its position in relation to the east and north-facing bank would seem to support this view (for notes on Wansdyke, see page 56).

From this high point it is worth taking in the view. There is a panorama stretching from the Georgian terraces of Bath, strung along and stacked upon the slopes of Lansdown in the west, to Brown's Folly standing above the dense woods of Bathford Hill to the east. Between these there is the limestone plateau of this southern fringe of the Cotswolds disected into isolated masses by rivers and streams, including the River Avon, Lam Brook, St Catherine's Brook and By Brook.

The Celtic field system of Bathampton Down can be seen well from this point too. Looking down the north-facing slope, the outlines of small rectangular fields are visible although the imposition of a golf course with its greens and bunkers has obscured the evidence somewhat.

Inclined plane As you descend the track from the old quarry on Bathampton Down you may notice some stone blocks with deep grooves embedded in them. These are the old stone sleeper blocks in which the iron rails of the tramway serving the quarry were set. This inclined plane system consisted of two lines – one by which loaded wagons descended by a rope and another by which empty wagons were hauled up the slope.

Track on Bathampton Down leading to Sham Castle

John Skinner (1772-1839)

John Skinner was born in Claverton in 1772 and served as curate there for a couple of years until the autumn of 1799. Two years earlier, as a newly ordained priest in holiday mood, he set off from his home village on a tour to Land's End and back. A selection of his voluminous journals was published under the title *Journal of a Somerset Rector* (John Murray, 1930). In addition, the present author edited and published Skinner's account of his tour in the west country (*West Country Tour*: Ex Libris Press, 1985). Skinner writes, of his first day's tour, September 20th, 1797:

'I left my Mother's house at Claverton, this evening, accompanied by Le Marquis de Kermel, a French Emigrant, designing to reach Wells to sleep, but we were detained the night at Old Down Inn, six miles short of our intended stage, by the rain. … The first part of the way from Bath, is very hilly, on a clear day, commanding extensive prospects on each side of the road; some gentlemen's seats beautifully situated in the vallies diversify the scene. … A communication has lately been made in the neighbourhood with the Kennet and Avon Canal, in order to convey Coal to Bath, and different parts of Wiltshire, an undertaking which promises considerable benefit to the Country gentlemen, as some of their estates, supply the commodity in abundance. …'

6 CLEY HILL

via Corsley Heath and the Whitbournes

Distance:	5 miles
Maps:	Explorer 143
	Landranger 183
Map Reference:	838444
Refreshment en route:	Royal Oak pub at Corsley Heath, about two-thirds of the way.
Note of caution:	It is necessary to cross the busy A362

Frome-Warminster road near the end of the walk. There is no danger if you wait for a suitable gap in the flow of traffic, though the 50 or so metres to walk until you leave the road can be slightly unnerving, especially if you have children with you.

THE WALK includes a number of field paths, tracks and lanes. Just inside Wiltshire, the country traversed has a definite Wiltshire atmosphere about it, with spacious fields and wide open vistas from the slopes of Cley Hill.

You descend from the chalk of Cley Hill to the greensand at Corsley Heath and the wooded hills of Longleat. There is a nasty road crossing on the very last leg of the walk which, unfortunately, is unavoidable.

Cley Hill is National Trust property and is approached from the A362 – the Warminster-Frome road. A signposted car park is provided a short distance from the main road. The view from the summit is well worth the climb, though it is not included in the route of this walk.

DIRECTIONS

To begin the walk, head up the track from the car park towards Cley Hill. Immediately past the barn make for the deeply sunken lane to the right. Follow this old way until the path forks – bear left

---

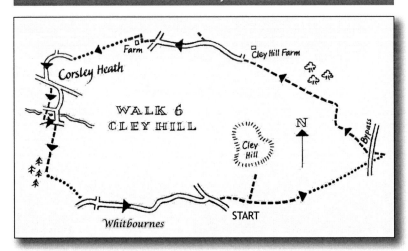

to reach a stile. Cross here and turn right to follow the hedgebank on your right. Cross the step stile into the next field and again follow the hedgerow on your right, then through a gap into a third field towards a steel gate close by the Warminster bypass. In the distance ahead you can see the wooded eminence of Arn Hill above the town.

Bear left along the concrete track and left again at the double steel gates where you turn left along the concrete farm track. Soon the concrete gives way to a grassy, fenced track.

When the fence ends you bear right towards the corner of the field, then left along the beaten track, following a course between hedgebanks. Where the track ends, continue in the same direction by following the narrow footpath which meanders through the undergrowth.

You reach a steel gate where you look down to **Cley Hill Farm** and beyond to the elongated, ridge-top village of **Chapmanslade**. Keep the fence on your left, then between fences, and head downhill until you reach the steel gate; go through here to reach another gate. Continue by the sunken lane opposite. Bear left when you reach the metalled lane. Eventually you meet a junction. Cross over and follow the track on the far side towards **Park Farm House.**

Turn right at the house and follow the boundary wall until you reach a stile at the point where it ends. Cross the stile and turn left. Now follow the path ahead in a straight line, looking out for a gate and stile to the left, then follow the beaten path as it heads across a field veering away from the fence on your right, towards the buildings of **Corsley Heath**. You head towards a kissing gate on the far side, the top rung of the wooden gate inscribed 'Donated by John E F Jones & Son'.

Follow the lane to reach the T-junction ahead. Turn left until you reach the main road at Corsley Heath. Across the road, a little to the right, is the **Royal Oak** pub. Cross the road and bear left. Look out for a Public Footpath sign beside a stile just before the former Corsley Post Office which still bears a post box.

Go through the kissing gate, this one inscribed 'In memory of Jack Brown', and soon another. Now follow the enclosed path and descend the slope to reach a further kissing gate, 'The Goodger Gate', at the foot.

Turn right at the lane and, after a few yards, sharp left down along a metalled footpath between cottages (**Whitbourne Moor**, according to the OS Explorer map).

Cley Hill

Do not go through the gate on your left but bear slightly to the right along the path between hedges opposite a coniter plantation. Cross the stream at the bottom and then follow the narrow way uphill to reach a kissing gate. Now bear left and head for the gate on the lane.

Turn left and then right at the junction ahead, up the concrete track. This soon leads to a green way between hedges. Carry on until the way levels out and you find a stile beside a gate (this one to 'George Sandy Sandwith, 1915-1998') in the fence on the left. Cross here and head across the top of this field just to the right of a conifer plantation, to reach a large open field. Carry on in the same general direction but a little to the right by the beaten path, just to the left of a steel farm gate, to reach a signposted wooden stile in the barbed wire fence.

Turn left on reaching the track, then straight across at the junction below – note the entrance to **Longleat Safari Park** to the right. This is a pleasant lane with little traffic and good views towards **CLEY HILL**. Continue by the NO ENTRY sign to reach the main road.

Cross the road here but TAKE GREAT CARE. The view in either direction is fairly restricted; use your eyes and ears to sense approaching vehicles and cross over quickly when there is a break in the traffic. If there are several of you together make sure you all cross at the same time, then carry on in single file.

Bear right and follow the grass verge for a mercifully short distance until you reach the entrance to a sunken way on the left. Head along here until you reach the hay barn near the car park and the starting point of the walk.

7 COMBE HAY

via Odd Down, Wansdyke, Southstoke and Rowley

Distance:	4 miles
Maps:	Explorers 142, 155
	Landrangers 172, 173
Map Reference:	734599
Refreshment en route:	The Wheatsheaf at Combe Hay;
	The Packhorse at Southstoke (if still in business)

THE WALK comprises an easy half day ramble. The route includes lanes, tracks, field paths, the Wansdyke and sight of the Fosse Way.

DIRECTIONS

With your back to the church in Combe Hay turn left up the hill. At the crossroads bear right along the lane signposted to Bath.

Notice the wall of engineering bricks immediately on the right. This forms the head of a tunnel of the former Camerton branch railway. If you look over the wall you can see the cutting; the line was tunnelled beneath the road junction at this point. The house to the left is tellingly named 'Tunnel House'.

Ignore a Public Footpath sign on the left by Cromwell Farm but, at the fork ahead, bear right and pass the cottage named '**Three Days**'. The considerable range of buildings on the slope to your left is Week Farm. A little farther on you pass **Fortnight Farm** to your left. Keep following the track uphill to a point where it swings to the right. Go through two gates on your left here into an asceding field and follow the beaten path beside a fence to reach a gate in the field boundary up ahead.

Before you continue onwards by the track through the woods, do pause

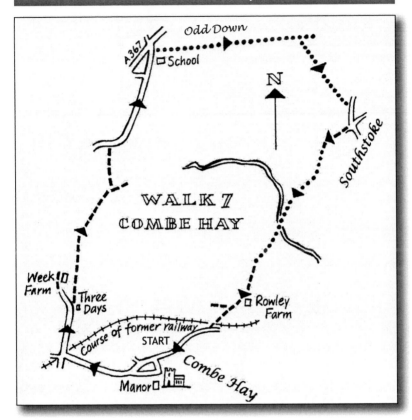

here and look back to enjoy the splendid view down the cleft in which Fortnight and Week Farms are situated. Beyond them is the valley of Cam Brook and, beyond it, the ridge which separates the Cam and Wellow Brooks.

At the junction of tracks and lanes above, walk straight on by the metalled road towards **ODD DOWN**. The long, low stone wall to your left forms the perimeter of a large car park which services the Bath Park and Ride scheme. Ahead are the roof-tops of Bath's southern fringe. You cross a road which leads past **St Gregory's Catholic College**, just beyond which look out for an iron gate and stile on the right.

Before passing through the stile notice the name of the road which crosses at the junction ahead: **'The Old Fosse Road'**. The modern road here follows the course of the Roman road before it descends to the ancient spa. Once past the stile take a look at the display board here with notes and diagrams explaining the **WANSDYKE**, a remnant of which you are now traversing.

The Wheatsheaf, Combe Hay

Once over the stile you follow the level path flanked by playing fields, the extensive, recently constructed 'Sulis Meadows' housing estate and agricultural fields. You are now traversing the plateau-like summit of Odd Down.

Continue along the ancient Wansdyke, pass through a kissing gate and continue beside an arable field to your right. You reach a metal kissing gate at the field boundary. Bear right here and follow the stone wall on your right towards the trees ahead. Carry on through the trees, across a drive, following which the path drops down to reach a lane. Bear right here until you reach the village of **SOUTHSTOKE**.

Facing the green bear right, past the church, farm and barn towards an indicated Public Footpath. Carry on through the kissing gate, heading downhill. A little way down, as the lane bends to the left, pass through an iron squeezer stile on the right and follow the beaten path downhill, past the house on your left. Keep heading down until you arrive at the stream at the bottom where there are footpath signs.

Bear right to cross the stream by the stepping stones – there are Public Footpath signposts on either side. The post on the far side (the last time I walked the route) indicates the **Limestone Link** route bearing half left. It heads uphill by the lightly beaten path. This is not very clear but if you head up towards the undergrowth you will eventually find a stile in the top left corner.

Cross over to enter a field and follow the beaten path not far from the hedgerow on your right to reach a kissing gate in the far right-hand corner. Pause here to take in the view – you may spot the tower of Southstoke church away to your left.

Once through the kissing gate bear left. Now follow the track with the hedge on your left; the track takes you to the buildings of **ROWLEY.** Beyond **Rowley Farm** you will be able to see the tower of **Combe Hay church** and, to its left, the dignified façade of Combe Hay Manor House. Follow the track downhill until you reach the lane – notice the entrance to **Caisson House** on the left and another former railway bridge.

Bear right on reaching the lane and gradually descend into the village. If you would like to visit the **Wheatsheaf** pub – and its garden is a delight on a fine day – you should keep your eyes skinned for a signboard on the right; the pub is in an elevated position, above the lane, overlooking the valley. You are now very soon back in **COMBE HAY** village.

BY THE WAY...

Combe Hay is a straggling village built on a south-facing slope which looks down towards Cam Brook. The village church, which has a small perpendicular tower, is at the southern end of the village, rather hidden behind the trees of the churchyard and close by Combe Hay Manor. If you venture beyond the semi-circular apse at the east end of the church you can see, over the church wall, the east façade of the manor house. The house is eighteenth-century, partly c. 1730 and partly c. 1770. The east façade, in sight here, is strictly classical, and very restrained. The Bath Stone used is particularly honey-coloured and is most attractive in the morning sun.

The church is fairly undistinguished, having been much restored in the nineteenth-century. Notice the stables which face the church across the churchyard; these Pevsner dates at c. 1700.

Wansdyke In parts, the Wansdyke can be seen to be a good ten feet above the level of the land to the north. The Wansdyke is a linear earthwork and occurs in two distinct parts – the East and West Wansdyke. The East Wansdyke is certainly the more impressive and traveres the ridge of the Marlborough Downs to the north of the Vale of Pewsey whilst the West Wansdyke runs in an east-west alignment south of Bristol and Bath, of which the way we are following is a fragment. The Wansdyke consists of a single bank with a ditch on the northern side, implying that it was built by a people living on the south side in defence against an enemy to the north. It is probable, therefore, that it was built by the Britons, under the command of Ambrosius and his lieutenant Arthur, against the Saxons.

Southstoke The little village green, marked by white railings and a bench seat, is a good spot to rest before the last leg of the walk back to Combe Hay. You will see the big house in the valley bottom just beyond the village. This is Hodshill and is, I am informed, the residence of a well known, ageing pop star (but I could not possibly say who).

Alternatively, you may seek refreshment at the Packhorse pub, which is by the road below the green. This interesting and unspoilt old hostelry has a seventeenth-century, three-gabled façade and an unspoilt interior so well worth a visit. The future existence of the Packhorse was in doubt the last time I was in the village so it would be worth checking before planning a visit.

Somerset Coal Canal The famous caisson lock on the Somerset Coal Canal is passed on the return leg of the walk from Southstoke to Combe Hay. Directly opposite this drive to Caisson House you can see a short stretch of the canal, now dry, but unmistakeable nevertheless. Just before you reach the road, you will pass by a brick wall like the one at Tunnel Farm House (at the start of the walk). This marks another former railway tunnel – if you peer over the top you will see the old cutting.

8   DUNDAS AQUEDUCT

• •

via Conkwell, Farleigh Wick, Pinckney Green and River Avon

Distance:	5 miles
Maps:	Explorers 155, 156
	Landrangers 172, 173
Map Reference:	783627
Refreshment en route:	The Fox and Hounds pub is at Farleigh
	Wick, the half-way point

THE WALK is almost entirely by field paths and green tracks and includes a delightful stretch of the Limpley Stoke valley beside the River Avon. This is a quiet and peaceful walk through woods and meadows and across hillsides with magnificent views.

Parking near the Dundas Aqueduct may be had in a lay-by beside the A361 – just beyond the garage on the right approaching from the south; but before the garage on the left approaching from the north.

DIRECTIONS

The canal and aqueduct can be reached from either end of the lay-by; a footpath leads down from the Bath end and a track from the other.

The wide basin marks the junction of the Kennet and Avon and the former Somerset Coal Canal which here began its journey to the Somerset Coalfield. It has been restored for a short stretch to provide mooring facilities for the growing number of craft using the K & A.

Cross the canal by the footbridge beyond the old crane (see picture on page 59), then cross the Dundas Aqueduct, a magnificent three-arched bridge which carries the K & A across both railway and river.

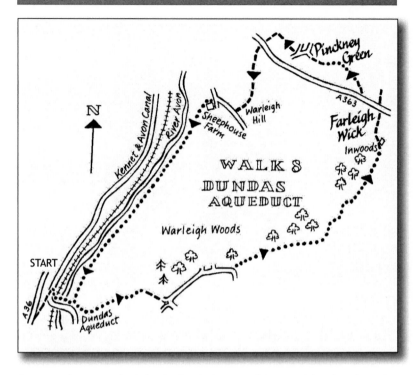

Once you have reached the far bank, keep walking straight ahead, to the left of the single-storey workshop and across a stile marked PUBLIC PATH. Immediately past the woodland to your left you leave the sunken way by climbing to a gap on your left by which you enter a sloping field. Head obliquely up and across the field to the top left corner to reach a stile beside a water trough. Continue in the same direction, with the wood to your right, towards the top left corner. Here you head uphill by a stony, sunken path.

You emerge at the hamlet of **CONKWELL**. Turn left at the top. At the T-junction ahead, signposted left to Warleigh, do not turn left but carry straight on. Just beyond the junction look out for a stone stile on the left. Cross here to enter a field where a far and wide view opens out; follow the path beside the wall on the left through a first field, then a further two where the path is enclosed by fences.

Crane and footbridge across the canal at Dundas Aqueduct

At the end of the third field, look out for a 5-bar gate where the fenced way bears to the right, go through the gate and keep the wood to your left, then a little to the right toward a gate and stile in the field boundary ahead.

Cross the stile beside the gate to enter a field all but surrounded by woods. Keep to the right and exit by a gate in a right-hand corner. Bear left in the next field towards a gate and stile. When you emerge from the woods, carry on in the same direction by following the boundary wall of Inwoods House on your left to reach a wooden kissing gate in the far left corner and the main road. This is **FARLEIGH WICK.**

Turn left, past the **Fox and Hounds** pub and **Midway Place**. Now cross the road with care and look for the Public Footpath signpost. This leads to steps down to a sunken way heading towards the hamlet of Pinckney Green. Follow this old way until you spot a yellow arrow pointing up the bank on the right. Scramble up here to reach an iron gate.

Follow the field boundary on your left and cross a stile beside a gate on your left marked by a yellow arrow. After a few yards look out for a kissing gate on the right similarly indicated. Go through here and ahead by the drive to reach a grassy triangle at a minor junction at **PINCKNEY GREEN**.

Bear left and cross the lane ahead to reach the drive signposted **16A**. Follow this drive for a few yards but then head in the same direction by the enclosed path which skirts the property's boundary to the right.

Follow this right of way until it bears left and leads you to the **Dry Arch** and under the main road. Carry on by the main path through the woods ahead (not over the stone stile on the right). Simply follow the main track through the woods, eventually taking a right fork where the path bifurcates.

You will enjoy glimpses across the valley towards Claverton. Press on until the path drops you onto the lane which runs between Conkwell and Warleigh.

Turn right and follow the lane until you reach **Sheephouse Farm** and an indicated public footpath. Turn sharp left here along the drive towards the farm, beside various outbuildings, then follow the arrows by bearing right along a fenced path. This takes you to a couple of metal kissing gates; bear left through the second one. Follow the beaten path down towards the river and then head upstream – the tree-fringed river bank to your right and hanging woods on the slope to your left – to reach **DUNDAS AQUEDUCT**.

Head towards the stile to the left of the boathouse beside **the Aqueduct** and climb up the steps to reach the canal towpath. From here retrace your steps across the aqueduct, cross the canal via the footbridge and up to the lay-by beside the main road.

BY THE WAY...

Conkwell At the bottom of its single street lies Spring Cottage; the spring can be seen in the hillside in front of the cottage. Other houses also tell a story in their names: there is Cromwell's Rest, where Oliver Cromwell is said to have rested between military engagements (it is also said that his men poisoned all the wells in the vicinity except that at Conkwell), and Old Bounds Cottage, which formerly marked the Somerset-Wiltshire boundary.

---

9 HOLT

via Great Chalfield, Little Chalfield and Merkins Farm

Distance:	4 miles
Maps:	Explorer 156; Landranger 173
Map Reference:	859617
Refreshment en route:	Holt has two pubs: The Tollgate and The Old Ham Tree. There is also the Glove Factory café in The Midlands, the Tea Room at The Courts (if you are amember of the National Trust) and Merkins Farm Tea Room (closed Mondays).

THE WALK is an easy one, using well-trodden paths, with no steep slopes. The route includes the magnificent medieval manor house of Great Chalfield. Parking is usually possible around Ham Green at the western end of the village and close to the two pubs, so this acts as the walk's starting point.

DIRECTIONS

Take the minor road which leads away from Holt's **Ham Green** towards the south-east (towards the church). This way takes you to the **Parish Church of St Katherine**.

Beyond the church bear left by a track which leads to a kissing gate and a footpath along the edge of a field.

You approach a pair of distinctive squeezer stiles (probably fashioned many years ago by the village blacksmith): one ahead and another to your left. Take the latter and follow the track to reach the main road through the village at the entrance to **The Courts**.

Before crossing the road notice the **United Reformed Church** buildings on the left; the older, plainer structure behind, with its pointed windows and hipped roof dates from 1810.

Cross the road, pass **Holt Village Hall** (former Holt Reading Rooms 1873, according to the inscribed stone tablet in the wall), and walk along the road called **The Midlands**. Bear right at the **Glove Factory Studios** (formerly Beaven's Leather Works, established 1770); walk past mainly industrial buildings but look out for the remains of the spa (see picture page 64).

Towards the end of The Midlands bear left, not into the recent housing development known as 'The Spa', but immediately to the right along a track to enter a field by a kissing gate. Continue straight ahead, ignoring the stile to the left. Walk on between hedgebanks as the field narrows. Go through the kissing gate and head up and across the next field, bearing very slightly to the right until you reach a further kissing gate at the top right-hand corner which takes you to the next field. Follow the hedgebank on your right a short distance and go through the next kissing gate. Great Chalfield and Mill Cottages are not far away across the field behind trees to the left.

Follow the hedgebank on your right towards a wooden footbridge to cross the brook below. Head half-left across the next field to exit into the lane at the far corner. Follow the lane beside the moat and fortified boundary wall of **GREAT CHALFIELD**, past the tiny All Saints Church and imposing manor house.

Continue the walk in the same direction along the drive past Great Chalfield House, past a bridleway sign indicating straight ahead to reach **LITTLE CHALFIELD**. Proceed along the drive – you may spot the distinctive saddle-back tower of South Wraxall Church a mile or so across the fields ahead.

An avenue of beech and horse chestnut trees takes you to a lane where you bear left, the left again at the minor junction below. Once over the stream in the valley bottom look for a Public Footpath sign on the right – ascend the right of way beside the hedgerow on your left.

At the top you cross a stile into the next field and continue in the same direction until you reach a lane opposite **MERKINS FARM**. Bear left if you wish to visit the café, otherwise turn right here and then left just past the first house you reach. Follow the indicated foorpath as it leads you into a field which offers a wide view south across the clay vale towards Salisbury Plain and south-west towards the spire of Bradford on Avon's Christ Church.

Walk on with the hedge on your left. Then, when the hedgerow takes a turn to the left, continue walking in the same direction to reach a stile in the far field boundary.

In the next field bear a little to the left towards a gap at the bottom left corner. Cross the following field to reach a stile and then another close to the pylon, following the hedgebank on your right. Leave this field and head straight on beside the hedgerow on the right; a group of farm buildings – Hunt's Hall Farm – appears across the field to your left. Reach a stile in the hedgerow ahead about twenty yards or so to the left of this field's right-hand corner.

Head diagonally across the next field, towards Holt, cross a plank bridge in the hedgerow about 50 yards to the right of the left corner, and head for the top left corner of the following field. Turn sharp left here and follow the beaten path which takes you to a lane where you bear right to return to Ham Green in **HOLT**.

BY THE WAY...

Holt Spa

As you walk along the Midlands look out for a surprise: beneath a wall at right angles to the road is an old pump set into the bricked-up entrance to a former well-house. The entrance is framed by a pair of Tuscan columns surmounted by a straight entablature. Below the stone is the following inscription: 'Sacred to the memory of Lady Lisle and the Revd. James Lewis, the persons who patronised this spring and rendered it famous in the year 1720'. This pump marks the site of a former spa which had ambitions to rival Bath.

Pump at Holt Spa

Great Chalfield House is a National Trust property which is open to the public on a restricted basis. It may also be familiar to you on account of its many appearances in films and television dramas. There is so much worth seeing in this late medieval manor house, in the church and grounds, that a visit is highly recommended.

10 LIMPLEY STOKE

● ●

via Midford, Pipehouse, Hinton Priory and Sharpstone

Distance:	5 miles
Maps:	Explorer 142, 155; Landranger 172
Map Reference:	784603
Refreshment en route:	The Hope and Anchor pub is at Midford, the half-way point; the Hop Poles pub is in Lower Stoke. There is also the excellent café in The Galleries in Freshford.
Note of caution:	It is necessary to cross the busy A36 twice; the first being on a fast stretch of road. There is no danger if you wait for a suitable gap in the flow of traffic though it is always slightly unnerving, especially if you have children with you.

THE WALK provides a variety of scenery and much of interest. There is a long descent from Limpley Stoke to the Midford Brook and a steady but fairly strenuous ascent from Midford to Pipehouse.

DIRECTIONS

The obvious starting point for this walk is Limpley Stoke parish church. However, parking in the vicinity is not possible so I advise leaving your vehicle in **Midford Lane** on the far side of the A36 (see map), where the road is wide enough to allow parking without causing an obstruction.

Facing the road, bear right past **Stoke Hill stone mine,** until you reach a forked turning where you bear right along a lane signposted **Old Track.** Quite soon there is a right-hand turning which leads towards more houses. Ignore this but go straight ahead by the unmetalled track to the left of a bungalow named '**Chatleys**'.

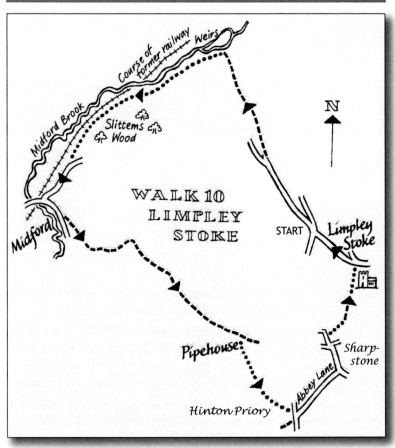

The track begins to descend, at first gently, then more precipitously. At the cross track below turn right, then sharp left, and continue the descent to the valley bottom. There are some good views from here towards **Monkton Combe**. The course of the old **Camerton Branch Railway** may be traced where it is marked by a level green sward on the far side of the valley, about 20 feet above river level; note too the saddle-back tower of Monkton Combe church.

As you reach the river you will see the former mill buildings ahead; these may be reached by a footpath which crosses the island lying between Midford Brook and the millstream.

But, to continue the walk, you bear left through the kissing gate before the bridge and follow the beaten path across the meadows beside the brook.

Follow this way for about half a mile. Soon after reaching **Slitterns Wood** on the slope to the left the path parts company with the river. The embanked course of the former railway crosses to the south side of the brook and forms a barrier between the path and the brook. Now continue along the valley slope with the embankment to your right, the wood to your left. You will pass through a series of kissing gates and finally a gap in the stone wall to reach a last field where a fourth kissing gate which drops you back into **Midford Lane**.

Before leaving this final field it is worth pausing to view the prospect across the valley. You will find yourself in full view of the singular and imposing façade of **Midford Castle**.

Bear right on reaching Midford Lane to reach the main road and the hamlet at **MIDFORD**. Turn right if you wish to visit the **Hope & Anchor** pub; otherwise cross the main road (with care) and bear left to follow a pavement for around 100 yards. You will find the start of the next stage of the walk in the shape of a gap in the hedge opposite, just past the **30mph sign**. Follow this old sunken way, mostly uphill, for about a mile.

You eventually emerge from the sunken way at a point where it widens and levels out – you will spot a water tower across the fields to your left. Bear right to soon reach the hamlet of **PIPEHOUSE**. Keep your eyes peeled for the former '**Village Room 1903**' (according to a tablet set in the gable wall). Directly opposite there is a stile opening on to an enclosed footpath. Cross the stile at the end and proceed in the same general direction via a number of gates and stiles, always keeping the ditch and hedgerow immediately on your right.

You will soon be confronted with a wide open field. Head directly across this to reach a stile in the middle of the boundary fence opposite. Climb over and now head in a half-left direction, to the left of the large, spreading, solitary tree and the gatehouse to **HINTON PRIORY**. Exit the field by a kissing gate to reach the main road, A36.

Cross the road, again with care, turn right and sharp left by **Abbey Lane**, signposted to Sharpstone and Freshford. Once past the entrance to **Homewood Park Hotel** you reach a gate and field opening (not our route) from where you should be able to spot the hill-top church of Limpley Stoke.

You begin to descend before the lane bears left; ignore the lane to the right (Rosemary Lane) and, at the crossroads below, go straight ahead (Ashe's Lane). This is **SHARPSTONE**, an outlier of Freshford.

After a few yards look out for an indicated Public Footpath on the right. Cross the stone stile, follow the drive until it bears right, and then keep to the footpath which continues straight ahead. There are three kissing gates and two more fields to cross before reaching **LIMPLEY STOKE** church. From here you turn left until you reach the A36, where you cross over (with care!) to reach your starting point.

You will spot the tower of **Freshford Church** below and to the right and will be surprised at how close together are Limpley Stoke and Freshford churches. You may also notice the solar array on the hillside which generates power for The Galleries shop and café in Freshford.

BY THE WAY...

St Mary's Church, Limpley Stoke is set high on a hill at the southern edge of Limpley Stoke far from the village centre. However, Limpley Stoke is built on various levels on the north-facing hillside: there is Lower Stoke, Middle Stoke and Upper Stoke, where the church is located, so it is difficult to pinpoint the village centre: the pub is in Lower Stoke, near the former railway halt, but the church is in Upper Stoke. The various levels are connected by a number of footpaths – notice the one opposite the church which is heralded by a handsome old stone squeezer stile and a badly chipped but evidently antique enamel notice.

St Mary's is an ancient church, as the Saxon arch (once a doorway) in the arcade testifies. We are told that behind the oak panelling in the chancel are to be found Roman tiles laid in a herring-bone pattern, the tiles having been recycled from a Roman settlement sited nearby. Also that the nave walls are believed to be those of a small chapel built in 1001 to mark the boundary of land given by Ethelred, son of King Edgar, to the Abbess of Shaftesbury in 973. Shaftesbury Abbey became the richest Abbey in England and was given the Manor of Bradford in 1001. The boundary between Somerset and Wiltshire, as well as that between the parishes of Limpley Stoke (in Wiltshire) and Freshford (in Somerset), passes through the field immediately behind the church.

St Mary's is a small, simple and unrestored church. It has a low, plain, unbuttressed tower surmounted by a short spire, partly hidden behind a parapet. The porch is early thirteenth-century with a round-headed arch and a statue of the madonna and child looking out of a niche above the door. Inside, in addition to the plain and narrow Saxon arch, there is a fine stone pulpit built into the north wall, Jacobean panelling on the balcony of the gallery and a font whose bowl is believed to be of Saxon origin. No list of the church's fabric can really convey the peace and charm of this ancient place of worship – do take time to soak in the atmosphere, it will do you good.

St Mary's Church, Limpley Stoke

Midford It is worth pausing here to take in the scene. Immediately on the right are the remains of the bridge which carried the Radstock branch line across the main road. A little further is the road bridge across Midford Brook together with Turnpike Cottage, and, just beyond the Hope and Anchor, the bridge which carried the Somerset and Dorset Railway (which replaced the former Somerset Coal Canal which also crossed here). Imagine what a busy spot Midford must have been in the heyday of steam!

Midford Castle dates from the late eighteenth century; the main house is constructed in the form of a triangle, with circular towers at each corner. According to an old guide book, the reason for this curious plan is as follows: 'A well known society gambler once made a fortune at the card tables by turning up the ace of clubs; in the hopes of perpetuating his good luck, he built this residence.' (*By the By-Ways Around Bristol*, 1927). Amongst recent owners were author Isobel Colegate and actor Nicholas Cage.

Hinton Priory is the ruin of a former Carthusian priory founded in 1232 and abandoned at the dissolution of the monasteries some three centuries later. The remains are scanty compared to the great ruined abbeys in the north of England, though the remains of the chapter house, sacristy, refectory and a small portion of the church and cloisters are visible, as well as the outline of the cloisters, which measure 226 feet square. The nearby village of Hinton Charterhouse commemorates the Carthusian connection in its name, and the Priory owned much of the land in the area. The hamlet of Friary in the valley between Freshford and Iford (Walk 1), is so named because it once comprised living quarters for lay brothers from the Priory.

It is possible to gain some good views of the buildings of Hinton Priory by following the right of way straight ahead from Pipehouse before turning left towards the gatehouse.

11 NORTON St PHILIP

via Hinton Charterhouse

Distance:	5 miles
Maps:	Explorer 142; Landranger 172
Map Reference:	774808
Refreshments en route:	The George and the Fleur de Lys at Norton St Philip; The Rose and Crown and Stag Inn at Hinton Charterhouse. There is also a small Post Office/shop in Hinton.

THE WALK is a pleasant and varied one which could provide an enjoyable half day's ramble or even a whole day.

The route leaves Norton by a field path and thence by a quiet lane through a delightfully unspoilt valley, then through a wood where it follows a track up a hillside. Now the route traverses a plateau at around 400 feet, with wide views north and south, for almost a mile before reaching Hinton Charterhouse. From Hinton Church field paths are followed for over a mile, back to Norton St Philip.

DIRECTIONS

To begin the walk: in Norton St Philip, with your back to the entrance of the **George Inn**, bear left. Take the left fork downhill but, almost immediately, cross the road and turn right along **North Street**.

At the end of **North Street** turn left by the lane leading downhill. Look out for a wooden stile beside a gate at **Lyde Green Cottage**. Cross this stile and then another into a field; head straight across the field towards a gap in the hedge furnished with a stepped gate in the far side. Cross into the next field and follow the field boundary on the left to reach a stile on the far side. Now head the short distance down and across the next field to reach a stile which drops you into a lane.

Turn right and continue along the quiet lane for about a mile.

Eventually you reach, on your left, a footbridge and ford across a stream. This provides a natural resting place.

Continue a little further by the lane until you arrive at a kissing gate and Public Footpath sign on your right. Enter Cleaves Wood and keep to the main, well-marked footpath, soon joined by a track from the right, which climbs the hillside.

Continue to follow the main track up the hillside until you reach a clearing; this is a peaceful spot indeed. Bear right here by a rising track below the wood on your right and exit the clearing by a pair of gates at the top. Head through the left gate and follow a wide track leading between fields.

As you approach a barn on your right the way continues in the same direction but now reverts to a narrow footpath between high hedges to reach **HINTON CHARTERHOUSE**.

The **Rose and Crown** pub is opposite; a shop and the **Stag Inn** along the road to the left. Cross the main road and continue by the lane opposite towards **Hinton church**.

The next stage of the route is indicated by a Public Footpath sign pointing across a stile on the right-hand side of the road, just before the turning which leads to Hinton church. Enter the field here by a kissing gate. Follow the beaten path to enter a fenced, linear plantation of mainly pine trees; follow the winding path until you reach the end and cross the stile.

Now head straight across the field to reach a strip of woodland. Soon the path veers to the right to skirt an overgrown sandpit.

Simply carry on by the main path through scrub and young trees to reach a wooden stile on the far side. Now head across this spacious field to the right of a wood. Bear left for a short distance to a gate which leads into the following field.

Bear a little to the right to walk beside a fence on your left, then tacking a little to the right to reach a gate.

Now follow the indicated way from gate to gate until you reach the access road to the farm.

Follow this lane for a short distance, keeping an eye open for a stile at the top of the bank on the left; this is found about twenty yards before the cottage. Cross into a field and turn right to cross the stile beside the cottage.

The right of way now follows the beaten path and heads diagonally across the field to reach a stile in the bottom left corner. The right of way here may not be obvious if there is a standing crop but rest assured that it plots a course diagonally across the field.

The gap at the bottom drops you onto the road which, bearing leftwards, carries you back into **NORTON ST PHILIP**.

BY THE WAY...

Norton St Philip is best known for The George Inn, that magnificent hostelry at the centre of the village which must have been photographed and sketched a million times. The George is said to have been built by the monks of Hinton Charterhouse and there is much of an ecclesiastical style about the detailing of the doors and windows of the stone-built ground floor. The inn was certainly used as a centre for the cloth trade; the top storey was once a great hall for the buying and selling of wool and cloth.

The George has its associations with the famous too – Oliver Cromwell slept here when in pursuit of Charles II; the Duke of Monmouth stayed over on his ill-fated expedition – he was actually shot at through the window of his room at the inn. Last but not least, Samuel Pepys ate and slept here and he records his satisfaction at doing so in his diary. The George Inn is a wonderful old building and it is well worth exploring the ground floor to which the pub user has access.

The view from the back of the George, where there is a garden, should also be savoured. The ground slopes down to a cricket pitch on Church Mead and beyond that is the church of St Peter and St James with its singular tower, said by some to have been constructed from fragments of the ruined priory at Hinton Charterhouse. There is a path on the right-hand side of the inn, as you face it, which leads down across Church Mead towards the church. Norton St Philip is a sizeable village which retains its school (still in its original building of 1827). There are many attractive, stone-built houses and the pavements are made up of irregular stone flags. Today, sadly, the Post Office and former shops have closed so that the village is quiet and unpeopled, though it is not difficult to imagine it in busier times.

Cleaves Wood At the outset we are informed that this is an SSSI – a Site of Special Scientific Interest, which basically means that nature here is left to her own devices. Early one May I found it alive with butterflies, especially brimstones and orange-tips, which seem to me to complement the English countryside better than the more exotic tortoiseshells and peacocks. There are also some good growths of Star of Bethlehem, especially near the summit and at the beginning of the open track to Hinton Charterhouse. Another plant which I failed to recognise was later identified as Chalkhill Milkwort.

Whilst on the subject of wild flowers, if you are walking in early summer,

Norton St Philip's two pubs stand opposite one another:
the George Inn and the Fleur de Lys

you may notice Bath Asparagus growing in the hedgebanks beside the lane before reaching the footbridge. The flowers are supposed to taste like asparagus; I remain unconvinced, though they are certainly edible and pleasant tasting and have long been something of a local delicacy. At this time of year you may be advised to take your pocket guide to wild flowers.

Path through Cleaves Wood

12 NUNNEY

via Lower Whatley, Egford, Vallis Vale, Great Elm and Whatley

Distance:	7 miles
Maps:	Explorer 142; Landranger 183
Map Reference:	737457
Refreshments en route:	The George at Nunney; sadly the Sun Inn at Whatley has now closed for business

THE WALK includes attractive footpaths beside streams and exhilarating stretches across fields. Sadly there is no streamside path between Lower Whatley and Egford and there is no alternative but to use the road for about a mile. However, this minor road provides a good vantage point across the valley of Nunney Brook. It is quieter at weekends with the absence of quarry vehicles.

DIRECTIONS

From Nunney Castle walk downstream beside **Nunney Brook**, past **All Saints Church** and the reconstructed **Market Cross**, and take the first turning on the left, **Donkey Lane**, making your way to **Combe Farm.**

As you approach the farmhouse bear right, through a kissing gate indicating the **Macmillan Way**, and follow the beaten path as it heads downstream, with Nunney Brook on your left.

You reach a junction of ways: turn left over the footbridge and right, leaving the Macmillan Way, at the stile on your right. Now follow the brook on your right.

At the bridge ahead climb up to the stony drive and follow it to the left past **The Grange Restaurant** at **LOWER WHATLEY.** As you head along the

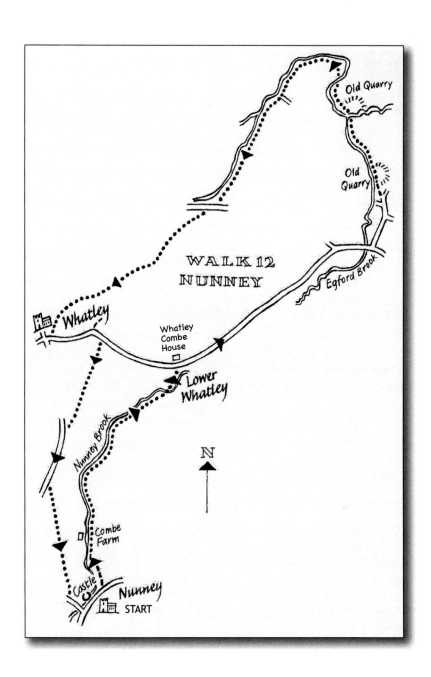

WALK 12
NUNNEY

Old Quarry

Old Quarry

Egford Brook

Whatley

Whatley
Combe
House

Lower
Whatley

Nunney Brook

N

Combe
Farm

Castle

Nunney

START

entrance drive look out for a signpost, with the message 'Please Keep to Footpath', in the shrubbery on your left. This leads to a wooden gate where you exit onto the road opposite a fine Georgian House (Whatley Combe House). Turn right and follow the road, past **Lower Egford Farm**, for about a mile.

Cross the brook (here known as Egford Brook) – note Zachary's Mill on your right – and turn left along Elm Lane. Pretty soon a lane joins from the right as Elm Lane bears leftwards; at this point head straight on by a track towards **Vallis Farm**. After 40 metres or so bear left by a fenced path. Soon you are back beside the brook; cross an iron stile to enter the wooded path along **VALLIS VALE**.

Continue to follow the footpath downstream until you cross a bridge by a confluence of streams. It is worth pausing at this point to follow the beaten path rightwards to reach an old quarry face (see note and drawing on page 83).

Carry on by the path, now upstream, and pass beneath two bridges, the second, larger one carrying the railway from a tunnel through the hill on the opposite bank. This modern section of the railway line represents a rerouting of the branch line serving Whatley Quarry.

Following the streamside path you will notice that the direction of flow is now against you, rather than with you. This is no longer the Egford Brook but the stream which flows from Murder Combe and Wadbury Valley and which unite at Great Elm, a little upstream.

Beside the footpath you encounter a number of old lime kilns which remain pretty much intact. The tops of the kilns project several feet over the base of the hoppers where the burnt lime was extracted.

Follow the track of the former line beside the stream until you reach the road below **GREAT ELM** via a kissing gate indicating the East Mendip Way. Cross over and pass through the kissing gate opposite. Two rights of way are indicated on the gatepost here: take the one which bears to the left. Climb the slope to reach a level footpath; bear right.

This is an enjoyable stretch along the edge of the overgrown valley with views over the quarried slopes towards the wooded hill on which the Iron

Age Tedbury Camp is sited.

The footpath emerges between two large, ivy-clad, Mendip stone boulders onto the road. Here you turn left for a short distance before continuing along the footpath indicated as 'Murder Combe Public Bridleway' by turning into the gap between hedges.

A gate leads to an enclosed path which soon reverts to a field boundary which you follow on your left. At the next junction you cross the stile to the left and follow the hedge on your right.

You will see the spire of **WHATLEY** Church ahead and feel assured that you are heading towards it. Your progress may be interrupted by explosions from the huge quarry on the far side of the valley to your right. There is a wide view, especially to the south-east, where you can see the plateau on which Frome stands and, beyond Frome, you can spot the distinctive outline of Cley Hill and the uplands of Longleat.

Follow the hedgebank on the right until you reach the top right-hand corner of the field where you cross a stile to your right into an adjoining field. Bear left to cross another stile. Ignore the stile to your left but head straight on to a further stile.

(The big house on your left is the old rectory. There is a ha ha between the house's front garden and the field; that is, a sunken wall and ditch which ensures that the view from the garden is unimpared but that beasts are confined to their field.)

Now bear left to cross the wooden step stile set into the fence, then carry on towards the wall enclosing **Whatley Church** where you will find a large stone slab stile which leads you into the churchyard.

Leave the church by the main gateway to the road and turn left. Follow the road towards a right-hand bend opposite Whatley Farm. Turn right towards the old Sun Inn, now closed for business. Head to the right of the old pub and to the left of the last house. Climb over the stile and follow a field path for about half a mile.

Bear just a little to the left, heading down the slope until you locate an old iron kissing gate in the bottom right-hand field corner. Head across the

Nunney Castle and moat, south side

following field to reach the road by a stile in the hedgerow on the right, about 50 metres before the far right-hand corner. Now bear left at the road, past **Southfield House.**

Carry on along the grass verge until you reach a dip marking the drive to Combe Farm. Don't enter here but carry on for just a few more metres until you reach a Public Footpath sign beside a stile in the hedge on your left. Climb over and head diagonally across the field until the far boundary hoves into view. Nunney about half a mile ahead: **Nunney Castle** with its great round towers is most prominent.

Make for a gap in the fence opposite and walk directly across the next field, beside a round pond and a solitary tree, with Combe Farm to your left, to reach a kissing gate. You now follow an enclosed path to reach the car park on the right or straight on for the village itself.

BY THE WAY...

Nunney is a gem, bypassed by the main road, its buildings grouped about the brook which flows towards the moat of Nunney Castle. The castle itself is a surprise in being built where it is – not in some easily defendable, hill-top position but sitting low in a valley. It is a ruin, but its four massive towers and curtain walls are pretty well intact, and the whole blends in remarkably well with the rest of the village and far from dominates the scene.

All Saints Church, opposite the castle, holds a more commanding position than the castle; it is situated on a gentle slope overlooking the village. The church contains much of the thirteenth and fourteenth centuries; perhaps its most notable features are the monuments to be seen in the north aisle. These consist of a knight and lady of the fifteenth century and another couple of the Elizabethan period. There is also a fourteenth century knight recumbent on the windowsill behind. These stone sculptures provide an interesting study in evolving fashion in armour, dress and hairstyles.

Vallis Vale Pictured below is one of several abandoned quarries in Vallis Vale. Such sites exhibit to perfection the horizontal Jurassic strata lying unconformably on the tilted Carboniferous rocks, the dramatic meeting point of two geological eras, tens of millions of years removed.

Quarry showing unconformity in Vallis Vale

Whatley Most of St George's Church is the work of the Victorian restorers, though there are traces of the original thirteenth and fourteenth century work. The church is generally kept locked. Close by is Manor Farm which has seventeenth century mullioned windows. The gatehouse, with decorated arch, is older still.

13 RODE

via Tellisford and River Frome

Distance:	3½ miles
Maps:	Explorer 143
	Landrangers 173, 183
Map Reference:	805540
Refreshments en route:	The Cross Keys pub and shop/café in Rode
	The Mill Restaurant/Bar at Rode en route

THE WALK completes a loop north of Rode by paths beside the River Frome, crosses an ancient packhorse bridge and climbs up through the attractive hamlet of Tellisford, to return via field paths to Rode Mill, now converted into a pub, and the village.

This short walk is strongly recommended. The quiet stretch from Langham House to Langham Farm is followed by Tellisford's ancient packhorse bridge and, in complete contrast, a recently installed water turbine harnessing the power of the River Frome. The climb uphill past old houses may be followed by a visit to All Saints Church.

There follows a series of field paths, sufficiently elevated to afford sweeping views down towards the River Frome in the valley below. Finally, there is the prospect of the former cloth mill at Rode, now a pub complete with revolving waterwheel, then the old bridge across the Frome, just wide enough to accept traffic in single file.

DIRECTIONS

The A361, though it passes close to Rode's parish church of St Laurence, bypasses the village, as does the B3109 to Bradford on Avon. There is usually space to park your car in the vicinity of the triangular village green with a war memorial at its centre and an attractive village sign.

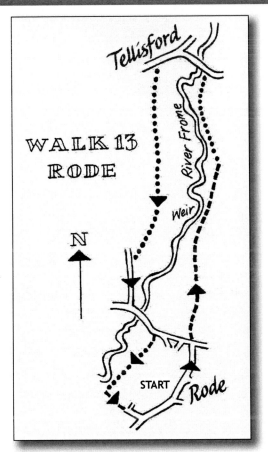

To begin the walk: From **Rode village green**, head northwards – via the village sign – out of the village, via High Street, slightly uphill to reach the main road. Cross over and head along the lane opposite, **Langham Place** (nos. 1 & 3 on the sign), beside the entrance drive to **Langham House.**

Continue by the metalled track as it follows the River Frome downstream towards Tellisford. Eventually the track forks – take the left fork, above the river, towards **Langham Farm.** Follow the right of way to the right of the farm buildings and enter the field beyond the gate. Now simply follow the river downstream, by a riverside meadow, a stile, a pill box and weir. You eventually reach another kissing gate after which you turn left to cross the packhorse bridge at **TELLISFORD.**

Continue the walk by climbing the slope by the flight of old stone steps. As you reach **Crabb Cottage** you might pause to look back up the valley towards the twin towers of Christ Church. Carry on climbing pass Crabb House and bear left onto the lane. The lane begins to level out as the tower of Tellisford's **All Saints Church** hoves into view. Look out for Lilac Cottage on the left and, immediately past it, an indicated Public Footpath.

Alternative short extension to visit All Saints Church:

Continue uphill. Once past **Top Farm** look out for a signposted stile on your right. Head straight across to reach a further stile, then bear left towards a massive stone stile in the churchyard wall. Should there be a standing crop here it may be as well to stick to the lane in order to reach the church. Retrace your steps to the field entrance beside Lilac Cottage.

Back on track:

The path now is rather elevated above the valley and provides a fine view down to the river and across the valley slopes on the far side. Follow the beaten path which gradually descends to reach a stile to cross a ditch. Stickers indicate that you are following the Mendip Ring.

Bear a little to the right to ascend a couple of terraces in order to reach a stile in the top right corner. Cross here and follow the hedgebank on your right. Cross a further two stiles, again beside the hedgerow and keeping the twin towers of Christ Church in sight.

At the third stile you change direction by turning right to follow the enclosed footpath. After the path bears to the right look out for a stile below to the left. Cross here and pass a bungalow to your left, then descend to reach a stile which drops you onto the lane. Turn left to reach the road by **The Mill** pub.

Turn left and cross the bridge, past a **The Miller's House** and a group of buildings with a Venetian window bearing the name **The Old Coach House**.

Bear right to reach the entrance to **Barrow Farm**. The gatepost here indicates the right of way. Walk along the drive and bear left via the enclosed path just before the farmhouse (not the kissing gate first seen). The path forks behind the house; take the right fork and follow this fenced path on an even contour just above the river.

A couple of kissing gates will take you to a cross-path where you turn left and left again at **Merfield Lodge** to reach **RODE**.

BY THE WAY ~

Rode The prospect back along Rode's High Street, with its rows of old houses, is an enticing one and you may like to begin with a short perambulation of Rode itself. To do so, head towards the village centre. Notice the old Baptist Chapel, dated 1780, and adjacent school room, dated 1839. Farther along, past the pub, in the vicinity of some former industrial buildings and set back from the street on the left, is a former Methodist Chapel, dated 1809. You can return to the village green by the lower street through the village by turning round and taking the left fork below the Cross Keys pub.

You might explore further by walking out of the village centre towards the old parish church on the A361. St Laurence dates from the fourteenth century though it was heavily restored by the Victorians. The clerestory windows and arcading make it a light and airy building. There is an interesting painting on display of the village men holding hands and dancing in a circle round the church. This ancient custom apparently had pagan origins, like so much of what is considered to be 'Christian tradition'. Known as 'clipping the church', it was enacted on Shrove Tuesday night for the avowed purpose of driving out the devil and survived in many parts of Wessex until the nineteenth-century.

Signpost on the green in Rode depicting scenes from village life through the years: the mill, the river Frome with the twin towers of All Saints Church in the distance and Fussell's Brewery which ended production in 1962, the bottling plant closing in 1992.

Langham House was formerly Rode Hill House, the scene of a mysterious murder in Victorian times. This story has been recounted often, most recently in *The Suspicions of Mr Whicher* by Kate Summerscale (Bloomsbury, 2008). For an alternative theory see 'The Unsolved Mystery of Rode' in a collection entitled *West Country Treasury* (Ex Libris Press, 1989).

Christ Church, Rode You will also certainly notice the twin towers of Christ Church, once Rode's second church, uphill to your right. This was erected in 1824 and is described by Pevsner as 'amazing'. It was made redundant some years ago and is now privately occupied and known as Christchurch House.

Tellisford This delightful hamlet features an ancient packhorse bridge and a state-of-the-art water turbine, on the site of the former Tellisford Mill, which harnesses the power of the River Frome to generate electricity. Tellisford is one of fourteen sites being utilised by Mendip Power, this one creating power sufficient for forty homes.

Tellisford's All Saints Church was much restored by the Victorians but is well worth a visit. As befits the small community it serves, All Saints is a diminutive building consisting only of tower, nave, chancel and porch and possesses an appealing simplicity. There are some interesting memorials within, including a couple to the Crabb family in the first half of the nineteenth century – we pass the eponymous Crabb Cottage and Crabb House on the climb up from the river.

The Mill at Rode was converted some years ago into a large pub, or 'Restaurant and Bar' as it describes itself. This former woollen mill stood empty and abandoned for many years until its reinvention as a watering hole. It is well worth a visit – sup a refreshing drink, see the huge waterwheel in the basement and gaze at the waters of the River Frome flowing beneath the undershot wheel. Records of a mill here date back to the sixteenth-century, though most of the present building was a factory erected around two hundred years ago.

The River Frome with Tellisford Bridge and fly fisherman;
Wiltshire to the left, Somerset to the right

14 SOUTH WRAXALL

via Monkton Farleigh, Farleigh Wick
and Great Cumberwell

Distance:	7½ miles
Maps:	Explorer 156; Landranger 173
Map Reference:	833648
Refreshment en route:	The Long Arms at South Wraxall
	The King's Arms at Monkton Farleigh
	The Fox and Hounds at Farleigh Wick;
	This ramble could turn into a pub crawl!
Note of caution:	It is necessary to cross the busy A363 twice;

There is no danger if you wait for a suitable gap in the flow of traffic though it is always slightly unnerving, especially if you have children with you.

THE WALK, though a good distance, does not entail any steep ascents. Most of the route is by field paths and green tracks, with a shorter section along lanes which carry little traffic. South Wraxall and Monkton Farleigh are both attractive and interesting villages. Navigation across wide open arable fields between Monkton Farleigh and Farleigh Wick, then from Farleigh Wick to Ashley Lane, can be problematic, particularly when fields are ploughed and planted without regard to rights of way.

DIRECTIONS

To begin the walk, make for the centre of South Wraxall, in the vicinity of the pub and church.

Head for the lane opposite the **Long Arms** pub beside the church. The lane eventually bears right: just after this bend look out for a turning on the left, beside **Willow Cottage**, and follow the track round towards the furthest cottage ahead. Follow the right of way to its left, climb a stile

---

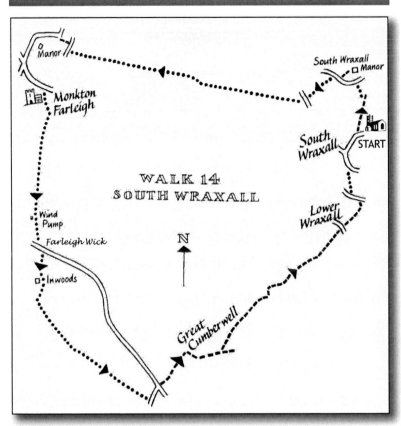

and follow the field boundary on your left to reach a further stile in the top left-hand corner – here you enter the lane running along the boundary of South Wraxall Manor.

Bear left along the lane for a short distance. Just past the farmhouse enter the field on the left by a kissing gate. Head directly across the field to reach the wooden stile in the opposite boundary – its whereabouts is at the point where the overhead cable meets the far side. Continue a short distance along the fenced path, then cross the next field to reach the lane by a gate.

The set of iron gates opposite originally formed part of the grand drive to the **Manor House** at Monkton Farleigh. Cross the wooden stile beside the gatepost and proceed to plod the one and a third miles along the wide, straight avenue to reach the lane below Monkton Farleigh Manor, whose

Georgian façade is clearly visible on elevated ground in the distance. You cross a couple of stiles en route to a final stile beside a cottage on the lane below the big house.

The most direct route from here to the church and village main street is to turn left and then right. However, there are things of interest to be seen by making a detour around the Manor's boundary. To do so, bear right.

Look to your right to enjoy a fine, distant view eastwards – on a fine day you will be able to distinguish the Devizes Downs (to the left) and Salisbury Plain, separated by the Vale of Pewsey.

Head past the entrance to Manor Farm and turn left up a lane until you reach a drive joining from the left. Opposite is a **Public Footpath** sign beside an attractive iron kissing gate. Go through here and make for the fenced enclosure nearby. Depending upon how overgrown this is, you may or may not be able to identify a body of water – a reminder of ancient monastic fish ponds.

Leave the fish ponds by the same gate and continue up the lane to bear left beside the boundary wall of the Manor. At the junction ahead you will find the famously haunted Kings Arms pub to the right. Bear left through **MONKTON FARLEIGH** village.

Immediately on the right, beyond the church, take the signposted **Public Footpath** to Farleigh Wick. This enclosed path leads to a step stile, a kissing gate and a stone slab stile. Cross the track and follow the fenced path to reach a junction.

Turn right here, keeping the hedgerow on your left. Pass through the kissing gate ahead to enter a field. Bear leftward to follow the hedge on your left until you reach a Footpath sign indicating the right of way beside the hedgerow on your right.

From the field edge the right of way heads across this wide field. Head straight for the **pair of white-painted gables** at **FARLEIGH WICK**. You find yourself passing to the left of an old wind pump. Look out for a stile on the left which leads to a second stile and cuts a corner to reach the exit from the large field in its far left-hand corner. Here you drop down onto the main road; the **Fox and Hounds** pub is just to the right.

Cross the road with care, bear left for a few yards. Just past the entrance drive to Inwoods, the footpath sign beside a wooden kissing gate indicates the way from here.

Follow the boundary of **Inwoods,** pass through a gate in the wooden fence and head towards a gate in the bottom corner. Now continue down towards a wooden stile in the hedgerow below. This is where navigation can be difficult. You continue by the gently ascending (sometimes) beaten track, very slightly to the left, to reach the opposite hedgerow where there is a gap and remains of a stone stile.

Go through here and cross the field in the same general direction. A crooked hedge faces you – head for the part nearest you which projects into the field; you will find a stile and crossing into the next field here.

Follow the hedgerow on your left for a short distance. Continue in the same general direction, again very slightly to the left but certainly left of the buildings up ahead on the horizon until you exit the field to drop down into **Ashley Lane,** at a point around 50 metres or so from the main road. You will see footpath signs on the opposite side of the lane which alas are not visible from the large field you have been traversing. Here bear left to reach the main road which you cross, but do take care.

On the far side to the right is the somewhat grandiose entrance to **Cumberwell Park Golf Club.** A little to the left is the drive which leads to **GREAT CUMBERWELL** Farm and this is our route. Head down here and turn turn right beside the high stone wall. This leads you past the former Great Cumberwell Farm – now converted into **Cumberwell Country Cottages.** The unnatural looking 'hills' to the right are the landscaped remnants of an extensive landfill site.

Bear left where the track forks and carry on towards **Cherry Orchard Farm,** from where the track leads directly to **South Wraxall.** A large lake has been created in the hollow beyond Cherry Orchard, no doubt forming the watery grave of many a misaimed golfball.

On reaching the lane at **Lower Wraxall,** cross over and continue by the way opposite which soon reverts to a footpath leading leftwards to a kissing gate and field. Follow the path to another gate and bear left by the sixteenth-century **Mison's Farm.** Cross the road to another well-marked path and through a further three kissing gates to **Church Fields** housing estate and the pub and church at the centre of **SOUTH WRAXALL.**

BY THE WAY ~

South Wraxall is a scattered village: the distance between the Manor House and the farm at the northern edge and Home Farm at the south is about a mile on foot and rather further by road. There are, in fact, three distinct nuclei to the village: the Manor House and Farm form a northerly group; the church and pub a central group, whilst Lower Wraxall comprises a number of farms, houses and cottages.

St James Church, South Wraxall

St James Church is most notable for its saddle-back tower with prominent stair turret. The tower dates from c.1300; Pevsner describes it as 'picturesque'. Inside, the church houses the Long Chapel, where generations of lords of the Manor of South Wraxall lie interred.

Pevsner says of South Wraxall Manor that 'the house is an outstandingly successful mixture of the fifteenth century and the later Elizabethan and Jacobean. Moreover, what features of both periods remain are outstanding in their own right.' However, the house is privately owned and not open to the public. The little that can be seen is certainly enticing: the gate house with immaculate oriel window over the archway, the enormous drawing-room window on the west front, which was added to the north of the hall in the late sixteenth-century and, in the garden facing the road, the domed, octagonal summer house. South Wraxall Manor was the home of the Longs from the early fifteenth-century until late in the nineteenth-century. It is said that the first tobacco smoked in England was smoked here.

Beyond the Manor to the east is the Manor Farm, the farmhouse of which was originally a hospice for poor travellers and dates from the fourteenth century. Little or nothing of this is visible from the road, however.

Monkton Farleigh The fish ponds at Monkton Farleigh were installed by the monks of the Cluniac priory of Monkton Farleigh, founded in 1125, and sited where the Manor House now stands. Little evidence remains of the priory, save a few stone fragments, a pair of lancet windows and some thirteenth-century stone effigies. None of this is visible from the road.

Once past the cottage on your right, you may see, at the far side of the field, a small, solitary building with a steep, pitched roof. This is the ancient Monks Conduit, where a supply of water was utilised to supply the priory and still does supply the Manor.

Monkton Farleigh's main street, with attractive mix of dwellings, leads to St Peter's Church which, apart from its thirteenth-century tower, was largely rebuilt by the Victorians. One unusual feature is the holy water stoop set into the wall at the entrance gate.

15 SOUTHSTOKE

via Tucking Mill, Midford and Somerset Coal Canal

Distance:	4½ miles
Maps:	Explorer 155; Landranger 172
Map Reference:	747613
Refreshment en route:	The Hope and Anchor at Midford, about half way

THE WALK is full of interest and variety, as well as much beautiful and unspoilt countryside, though we are never very far from the southern fringes of Bath. There is a steady descent from Old Midford Road to Horsecombe Vale and a sharp ascent back to Southstoke at the end of the walk.

DIRECTIONS

To begin the walk: as you face the green in Southstoke turn left by the lane which leaves the village in an easterly direction. After about a quarter of a mile look for a gap in the hedge on the left where a signposted public footpath leads through a kissing gate and across a field to a gate in the far right-hand corner.

Cross **Old Midford Road**, then the main road with care and make for the signpost and kissing gate opposite. Enter the field and descend beside the hedgerow on the left-hand side, passing through two kissing gates. Following the second gate bear a little to the right towards a gap in the hedge. Pass through here and proceed to the stream below. This is **Horsecombe Vale**. Pass through the kissing gate, cross the stream and bear right.

Notice the boundary stone on your left, dated 1894, which marks the boundary between Somerset and the City of Bath.

Follow the path along the valley, slightly above the stream, first through woods. You emerge to find a group of buildings before you. These form part

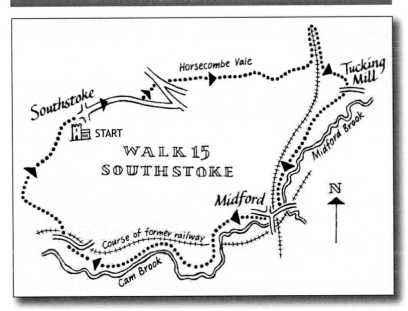

of the **Wessex Water Authority**'s complex at Tucking Mill. Cross a stream flowing from the left. At this junction of paths, it is worth making for the tall kissing gate which leads onto the recently created **Sustrans cycle route** on the trackbed of the former Somerset and Dorset line – if you look left you will see the entrance to the tunnel beneath Combe Down.

Back at the junction of paths, take the path leading directly up the slope, parallel to the cycle route until it enters the tunnel. At the kissing gate bear right and right again to follow the path which runs parallel to the cycle path.

Now begin to head downhill, following the course of the former railway track until it veers away to the right. Enter a wood by a kissing gate. The path continues along the side of the cutting, above Tucking Mill reservoir, and finally beside a house on the right until you reach a lane.

Here you turn right and, almost immediately, enter the right of way just to the left of the hedge indicated with a **Public Footpath** sign at ground level. This group of dwellings comprises **TUCKING MILL**, formerly a scene of some activity, in particular the extraction and processing of Fuller's Earth which outcrops in the vicinity.

Notice the house across the lane on your right - its front wall bears a tablet commemorating the fact that William Smith lived here - see feature on page 101.

Now simply follow the beaten path, which soon follows the towpath of the former **SOMERSET COAL CANAL**, through the undergrowth until eventually you emerge at the main road at **MIDFORD**.

On reaching the main road at Midford turn right. The next stage of the route is indicated by a Public Footpath signpost opposite the **Hope and Anchor** pub.

Follow the footpath beneath the viaduct. Pass through the wooden kissing gate and you soon emerge into the open; once again you are following the towpath of the canal. You will notice a stone bridge on the left - this marks an aborted southerly branch of the Somerset Coal Canal.

You must now pass beneath the railway bridge over the Cam Brook. Go through the kissing gate ahead and bear left towards the stream, then right along the water's edge and under the railway bridge. Bear right beneath the bridge, then left after a wooden kissing gate to continue the walk along the old canal towpath.

This section of unspoilt countryside is the most rewarding of the route. Following prolonged wet weather the canal bed becomes flooded and really looks like a canal.

Further along you encounter a series of three locks, the stonework now fairly dilapidated and overgrown. After the third lock the towpath reaches a kissing gate. Go through and turn right, Immediately look out for a gate on the left; cross here and follow the enclosed path towards the buildings ahead. Bear right to reach the lane by a kissing gate. Cross the lane and head under the brick railway arch opposite.

Here is an interesting plaque which relates the history of the Coal Canal, in particular the various attempts which were made to overcome the problem of raising barges at this point.

Follow the canal towpath once again, keeping the basin and locks to your left. Following five such locks, the canal takes a hairpin bend to the left through the woods.

To return to Southstoke, go through the kissing gate ahead and follow the path, keeping the stream on your left. The path bears right to ascend the hill, passing to the left of a house, then along a track by the edge of a wood.

Pass through an iron squeezer stile, then climb the field ahead to reach a similar stile at the top. This drops you onto a lane which leads directly to **SOUTHSTOKE** – the barn, the church and the green in the village centre.

BY THE WAY ~

Southstoke is an attractive village set in a hollow between Odd Down and Hodshill, its buildings well grouped around the crossroads and small sloping green at its centre.

St James Church has a low perpendicular tower; its main feature of interest is its intricately carved Norman doorway. The carvings appear rather too crisp, probably indicating work carried out during the restoration of 1845 – indeed, the entire right-hand pillar was replaced at that time. Sketches on display inside show the church after the 1712 rebuilding and before and after the 1845 makeover.

Beyond the church is Manor Farm and barn. The barn dates from c. 1500 and incorporates a dovecote beyond the central porch.

Somerset & Dorset Railway and Cam Valley branch line: The Someset & Dorset, which linked Bath and Bournemouth, was known as the 'S & D' and sometimes the 'Slow and Dirty', and operated for best part of one hundred years until 1966. The section from the former Green Park Station in Bath south to Midford now comprises the Two Tunnels Greenway and has been adopted by Sustrans and converted into a dual walking and cycling route.

The Camerton branch line opened in 1910 to provide a link between the Somerset coalfield and the main line from Bath to Weymouth at Limpley Stoke. The Somerset Coal Canal closed in 1898 after a century of service and the railway more or less followed its route but enjoyed a much shorter life, finally closing in 1951 following the closure of the Camerton Pit.

The two disused railway viaducts at Midford are like a couple of stranded dinosaurs of the railway age. The larger one beside the pub, which still spans the road, carried the Somerset and Dorset line from Bath, whilst the smaller, which no longer spans the road, carried the Cam Valley line from Limpley Stoke.

Somerset Coal Canal: About half-way along the section between Tucking Mill and the main road at Midford, at a point where a clearing allows access from the lane on the right to the field on the left, the prospect changes. The embankment of the old Somerset & Dorset Railway can be seen on the far side of the lane to the right.

The fact that you are following the towpath of the old Somerset Coal Canal is shown by the recognisable cross-section: to your left is a man-made embankment which drops away to the Midford Brook whilst to your right is the shallow basin of the canal. As you draw close to the main road you may notice fragments of old engineering bricks dumped on the opposite canal bank – these are surely the remains of the bridge of the former Camerton branch railway which once spanned the main road beyond.

One of a succession of five former locks

Bridge over the disused canal, beyond Midford

The Midford Brook from Midford itself down to the Avon marks the former boundary of Somerset and Wiltshire, so that Limpley Stoke and the hill behind are in Wiltshire.

As you follow the former canal towpath from Midford you will see a rather grand bridge over the Cam Brook to the left. This marks the course of an aborted branch of the Somerset Coal Canal: this was as far as it got. Farther along, just before the railway embankment, which is built across the canal and completely blocks it off, there is another stone bridge looking very forlorn as it spans a dried-out and grassed-over canal bed in a cow field (illustration opposite).

William Smith (1769-1839)

William Smith lived at Midford when he was employed as engineer on the Somerset Coal Canal. Smith became known as the 'Father of English Geology' because he it was who recognised the orderly succession of strata in the earth's crust and that each layer may be identified by the fossil remains it contains. Smith went on to conduct a geological survey of the country around Bath and drew some of the first geological maps, including the first one of the whole country. William Smith's fascinating story is related in a very readable book by Simon Winchester (*The Map that Changed the World*: Viking, 2001) – highly recommended. The interested reader may also care to refer to *The Geology of Somerset* (Ex Libris Press, rev. ed. 2011) by former Bristol University lecturer Peter Hardy. In his account Hardy makes the point that, contrary to the plaque noted, it is believed that Smith actually lived in the house behind, about 50 yards to the north, which we pass on the footpath down from the railway tunnel entrance.

16 St CATHERINE'S

via St Catherine's Valley

Distance:	3½ miles
Maps:	Explorer 155
	Landranger 172
Map Reference:	777703
Refreshment en route:	Alas, none

THE WALK begins in the valley at St Catherine's Court where the group of buildings includes the big house, the tithe barn and the church (which alone is open to the public) and soon climbs a lane to reach a plateau. There follow hedged tracks, field paths, wooded stretches and inspiring views. The whole area, no more than two miles from the centre of Bath, is deeply rural and could be a hundred miles from a place of any size. Parking on the lane in St Catherine's Valley is limited. The lane widens near the Court and it is advisable to park under the trees before the Court gates are reached.

DIRECTIONS

To begin the walk, make for the kissing gate on the right, just beyond the entrance to **St Catherine's Court**. Go through here to enter the field which reaches down to **St Catherine's Brook**. Head diagonally – half-left, just to the right of the telegraph pole – across the field, by the beaten path, until you reach a wooden kissing gate in the hedgerow as it descends to the brook.

Cross here and head down towards the footbridge at the bottom of the garden. Cross the stile opposite. Bear left and follow the beaten path upstream, above the trees.

You cross a stile to reach a path, signposted '**Limestone Link**' which carries

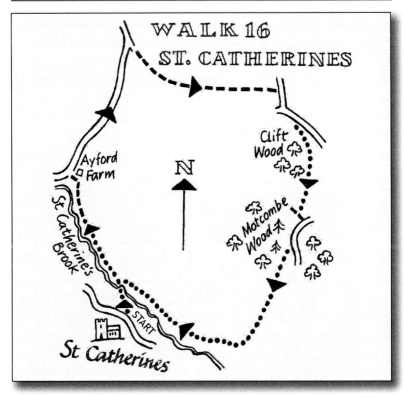

WALK 16
ST. CATHERINES

Ayford Farm

N

Clift Wood

Motcombe Wood

St Catherine's Brook

START

St Catherines

you across a tributary stream flowing from the right, then over another stile to follow the same tributary upstream. The right of way now forsakes the stream by bearing left by an enclosed path to reach the lane where you turn right, past **Ayford Farm**. The lane now climbs, quite steeply.

This is the best kind of country lane – deep sunken; vegetation trying to force its way through the centre; much growth on banks that the hedge-cutter does not seem to reach until the summer's end – and scarcely a hint of traffic. Look out for the occasional gates on the left which allow long views westwards.

Carry on until the lane begins to flatten out and keep your eyes skinned for a bridleway on your right. When you spot it you turn sharp right and follow this enclosed track above a steep slope at the head of the valley. The Gloucestershire village of Marshfield is only a mile across the Cotswold plateau to your left. The track eventually becomes more open but continues in the same direction beside a field boundary on your right.

You emerge onto the lane: turn right to follow the lane past the entrance to **Motcombe Farm**. Immediately past **Ashwicke Home Farm** you reach an indicated footpath leading into the field on your right. Go through the kissing gate here and bear left to follow the beaten path through the field, descending a little, above the hanging woods to your right to reach a kissing gate in the far bottom corner.

At a junction of paths, carry on to emerge into the open at a bulbous promontory which is a perfect place to sit and stare. With a far view along the valley flanked by thickly wooded slopes you begin to feel that here you are truly in the foothills of the Cotswolds.

Climb directly down the steep hillside, following the same general direction. The path is clear where it heads for a gap in the wood below. Pass through the kissing gate, then bear left to reach the lane.

Turn right at the lane. After a hundred yards or so, look out for a steel gate, indicated as a right of way, on the right. Cross the stile beside the gate, then another a few yards further on.

Now follow the beaten path beside a dammed pond towards a stile indicating a permissive path beside the hedgerow on your left. As you draw near the house ahead bear right towards a stile in the field corner. Once through here bear half-left to reach a stile in the hedgerow below; St Catherine's can be seen on the far side of the valley to the right.

Follow the valley upstream, gradually bearing left. Cross a couple of stiles to reach the footbridge across the brook at the bottom of the garden which you negotiated at the start of the walk. Simply retrace your steps back to the lane at **ST CATHERINE'S**.

BY THE WAY...

St Catherine's was originally a possession of Bath Abbey, the Court and church being built in the late 1400s. The present building is said to date from the fifteenth-century, with the exception of the library wing and the orangery, which were added in 1919 but built in the original Tudor style.

St Catherine's Church contains a representation of Prior Cantlow in the fine stained glass dated 1490. There is an impressive monument to William Blanchard (died 1631), and his wife, in the form of two life-sized kneeling figures on the north side of the chancel. The whole group at St Catherine's – the Court, the church and the tithe barn – forms a delightful ensemble, the weathered stone of these attractive old buildings set against the green, wooded hillside. The best view is perhaps from the footpath below, approaching from the south, a point included in the route of this walk.

St Catherine's Church seen through the gateposts to the Court

17 STEEPLE ASHTON

via East Town and Stourton Water

Distance:	4 miles
Maps:	Explorer 143
	Landranger 173
Map Reference:	905571
Refreshment en route:	The Longs Arms in Steeple Ashton

THE WALK is an easy half day's ramble with no steep climbs. It passes through open, arable fields and affords some fine views towards Salisbury Plain. Interest is added at the half-way stage at Stourton Water, a large pond fed by a tributary of the Biss Brook and a haven for wildlife.

DIRECTIONS

There is usually space to park in **Church Street**, just off the main street through Steeple Ashton. If you are starting from the church, you should head back to the main street, turn left and carry on past the village green and the pub. Ignore the public footpath sign indicating a right of way to the right, just past the pub, but walk on a few metres and turn right into **Acreshort Lane.**

Walk along here until the bungalows give way to fields and views onwards towards the escarpment of Salisbury Plain and the villages along its foot. After half a mile or so you reach a junction of ways where you turn right by the track signposted as a bridleway leading to East Town Farm. Follow this hedged track, first down, then through a dog-leg bend right and left, and up again towards **EAST TOWN** Farm, easily identified by its wind pump.

Walk through the farm buildings and past the cottages to reach the

lane where you bear right. You can see, to your left, across the grounds of Rood Ashton Park.

Follow the lane down to a dip where willows and reeds grow and the lane crosses a brook by a bridge. The wooded area to the left is **STOURTON WATER**, the presence of water hinted at by the fishing notices hereabouts. Here is a junction of ways – to the right is Sandpits Lane leading back to Steeple Ashton; straight on is **Mudmead Lane**, a Restricted Byway and the next stage of the route; to the left is an indicated right of way to Trowbridge.

It is worth bearing left here by the indicated Bridleway for 50 yards or so until a gap in the hedge affords a lovely view across Stourton Water towards the island at its centre. You are almost certain to see herons and, with luck, a kingfisher or two.

Continue in the same direction by the hedged but unmetalled track which climbs out of this dip, straight ahead.

You quite suddenly emerge from the undergrowth to witness a wide view south-eastwards across the fields towards the village and the escarpment beyond. Carry on – the track levels out and eventually reaches a section which is evidently used by wheeled vehicles.

Look out for the public footpath sign along here and turn right by a gate. Walk directly ahead and continue in the same direction towards a low brick building indicated on the Explorer map as 'Reservoir'. Make for a stile just beyond the left-hand side of this building. Cross here and follow the field boundary on your left. You reach a stile beside a gate on your left – cross here to enter built-up Steeple Ashton. Turn left at the T-junction ahead and you very soon reach the main road.

You can reach the village centre by simply turning right, but there is a pleasanter way back to the church by crossing the road and climbing the stile opposite. From here you cross the field towards the church and head for the road by the passage which is found beside the church wall on the right. Or simply carry on to the centre of **STEEPLE ASHTON.**

BY THE WAY...

Steeple Ashton is one of Wiltshire's most attractive villages and one of its best conserved, as the plaques opposite the village green which record several successes in the Best Kept Village competition testify.

The church is stunning: its numerous pinnacles leap up like so many exclamation marks and compel the passer-by to gaze long and admiringly. St Mary's is a large and magnificent church and a reminder of the great prosperity which the wool and cloth trade brought to this community in the past. Inside the church there is stone vaulting in all parts but the nave, which has a wooden roof. The steeple, which formerly reached a height of 186 feet, collapsed in 1670.

In addition to the church, this sizeable village exhibits a collection of houses notable in the variety of periods, styles and building materials they exhibit. There are houses built of stone, but also of brick; there are some of both materials. There are one or two stone roofs, but more of tile or slate or thatch. There are cruck-built cottages, timber-framed houses and scaled-down Georgian town houses. There is a village green with a blind house and a village cross, dated 1679, with a sundial.

The village green, Steeple Ashton, featuring market cross and blind house

Stourton Water Before heading on by Mudmead Lane, it is worth crossing the stile into the field on your left in the direction of Trowbridge. A few yards along you will be rewarded with a glimpse of Stourton Water. This is a beautiful stretch of water and a good place to stand still and wait for the wildlife - you are almost bound to see the fish jumping and a kingfisher or two flash silently above the water. The muddy banks of this little lake are also a good place to look for those plants which prefer such a damp habitat.

Mudmead Lane This is the sort of old byway where one half expects to come across an encampment of gypsies. Indeed, the extension of this lane on the far side of Steeple Ashton is named on the Explorer map as 'Gipsies' Lane (Track)'. Wild flowers prosper in Mudmead Lane – with one species dominating for a stretch, then another (there is a vigorous growth of comfrey in the lower reaches) – as do the butterflies when conditions are right. These old, sunken, and half-forgotten ways act as a kind of linear nature reserve nestling among the vast, prairie-like fields which surround them.

18 UPTON SCUDAMORE

via Norridge, Chapmanslade and Thoulstone

Distance:	6 miles
Maps:	Explorer 143
	Landranger 183
Map Reference:	865477
Refreshment en route:	The Angel Inn in Upton Scudamore;
	Three Horseshoes in Chapmanslade

Note of caution: It is necessary to cross the busy A36 twice. There is no danger if you wait for a suitable gap in the flow of traffic though it is always slightly unnerving, especially if you have children with you.

THE WALK is a relatively long one along old tracks and field paths, with a little road walking. There is a real sense of remoteness from the workaday world along much of this route. The field paths and tracks from Norridge Farm to the lane below Chapmanslade are a delight and the thickly enclosed track which stretches from Thoulstone Farm to the lane near Upton Scudamore, with occasional glimpses over wide, empty corn fields, has a real touch of mystery about it.

DIRECTIONS

Outside the church the road is wide enough to allow parking. With your back to Upton Scudamore church turn left along the lane and carry on until the road swings away to the right. Make for the metal kissing gate and signpost at this point. Head straight across the field, aiming for the walls of a stone bridge across the railway. It is worth pausing en route to take in the wide view and plot your course ahead. The wooded eminence of Arn Hill is to your left, the Warminster bypass below, the wooded grounds of Longleat, the isolated knoll of Cley Hill, Norridge Wood and Clear Wood ahead on the far side of the A36.

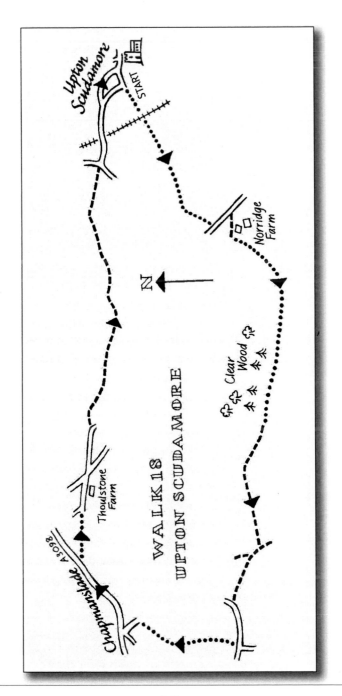

WALK 18
UPTON SCUDAMORE

111

Your way is straight ahead, first across the old bridge over the railway, then in the same direction. At the end of this field cross the footbridge and once again carry on in the same direction. Cross the next stile ahead and follow the field boundary on your right.

At the end of this field you cross a plank bridge across a ditch to access the stile above. Now head diagonally across this last field to the far left corner to reach a step stile. Cross here to reach a redundant stretch of the A36. Turn left and climb the step stile beside the gate to reach the road. Cross over (with care!), bear left and head along the grass verge to reach **NORRIDGE Farm.**

Turn right into the farm and follow the concrete track through a gate and past the farm buildings to a point where it bears left, just before a white painted wall and entrance to a driveway, then through a couple of gates to enter a field. Follow the wheel tracks diagonally across this field to reach the far right corner. Take the gate on the right leading into a long narrow field. Follow the field boundary on your right until you leave the field to follow a wide track with **Clear Wood** on your right and a hedgerow on your left. You eventually emerge into a field where you follow the hedgerow on your left.

Now you can see Chapmanslade village – a long line of buildings standing prominently on the ridge about a mile to the north-west. The western tip of Chapmanslade is in Somerset; Frome is about three miles further west.

Simply follow the hedgerow on your left, descending slightly, until you reach a hedged track below, then an open field and, once again, an enclosed track. Bear right when you reach the cross track indicating Public Bridleways.

A little further on there is a junction of tracks: take the left fork and follow this until you reach the lane beside a barn. Turn left here.

Follow the lane until you can see a post box on the triangle ahead. Just before this look out for a drive to Rosebank House on your right leading to a narrow path uphill beside a fence.

Climb the stile at the top and cross the field to reach the stile in the fence further on. Head in a half-left direction to a far corner of the field where you will find a stile. Now follow the beaten path to reach the track where you turn left past houses to reach a triangle at the road through **CHAPMANSLADE**.

Turn left if you want the village pub but right to continue the walk. There is a pavement on the left. Once beyond the buildings, first the pavement, then the grass verge, peter out. A little further on you climb the stile on the right and cross a field to reach **THOULSTONE Farm** by heading just to the left of the farm buildings. Here you exit the field by a wooden step stile. Follow the road to the right.

Cross the A36 (again, with care).

Head along the drive opposite, signposted **Thoulstone Park Nurseries.** At the point where the metalled road veers off to the right, you bear left along a stony track which is signposted as a bridleway. The now defunct Thoulstone Park Golf Club occupied the large building to your left. Quite soon the chippings abate and the track becomes a lovely green tunnel leading back between fields towards Upton Scudamore.

You eventually emerge at a junction of lanes. Cross over and take the lane opposite which leads across the railway line directly to **UPTON SCUDAMORE** and the village church.

BY THE WAY...

Upton Scudamore is so named because it is situated some four hundred feet up on a spur of lower chalk which juts out to the west from Salisbury Plain; the Scudamores were lords of the manor since Norman times. The village church of St Mary was largely rebuilt by the Victorians, and the plain tower a century before, although it does retain a good Norman arch. There are few buildings of antiquity in this rather workaday village though the Manor Farmhouse is partly medieval.

Chapmanslade is built on a ridge formed by an outcrop of Upper Greensand. The place name Chapmanslade literally means 'the road of the chapmen', or pedlars, and one can imagine the long road crossing the county boundary and linking Westbury and Frome being a favourite meeting place for traders.

Dead Maids Cross The house at the junction to the left is known by the unusual name of Dead Maids. The origin of this name lies in a rather gruesome story which begins in Black Dog Wood, a little to the north. A local farmer's daughter had two suitors, each unknown to the other, one of whom owned a black dog. When they discovered each other's intentions the two men fought until the owner of the dog was killed. At this the dog killed his master's slayer and the farmer's daughter committed suicide and was buried at Dead Maids Cross (according to Kathleen Wiltshire in her book, *Ghosts and Legends of the Wiltshire Countryside*, 1973).

Old granary, Thoulstone Farm, near Chapmanslade

Thoulstone An interesting feature at Thoulstone is to be seen on the left of the drive just beyond the farmhouse. There is an old granary still intact: a wooden structure standing upon staddle stones. Staddle stones are, of course, a favourite item of garden furniture and one can find them in many pub and private gardens in the countryside. But here they are still in their original position: supporting a wooden granary and protecting grain, once stored here, from vermin.

19 WELLOW

via Baggridge Hill and Stoney Littleton Long Barrow

Distance:	6 miles
Maps:	Explorer 142; Landranger 172
Map Reference:	741583
Refreshment en route:	The Fox and Badger in Wellow

THE WALK is fairly energetic but offers some great views and has a surprisingly remote feel. The route leaves Wellow to follow the Wellow Brook downstream, then heads up a tributary valley towards Norton St Philip, branching off to climb Baggridge Hill. A walk along its ridge is followed by a descent through a wood, then by bridleway and footpath, via the spectacular Stoney Littleton Long Barrow, to return to Wellow.

DIRECTIONS

To begin the walk, take the lane, **Mill Hill,** leading down beside the village school past the twin pillars which supported the former railway bridge, towards **Wellow Brook.**

Just before the ford, look out for a kissing gate on the left: cross over here to enter a field. Wellow Brook meanders its way down the valley to the right – simply follow the general eastward course of the brook without sticking to its every twist and turn.

Cross the field to reach a gate, then follow the track between barns. In a further field bear right and look out for a footbridge to cross Wellow Brook.

Once across, the right of way climbs the field diagonally to the left to reach a gate below the row of trees. There are some splendid views hereabouts up and across the valley. Go through the gate and head in the same direction to reach a gate in the hedgerow. Cross here and follow the hedgebank on your right to reach the lane opposite **Wellow Farm.**

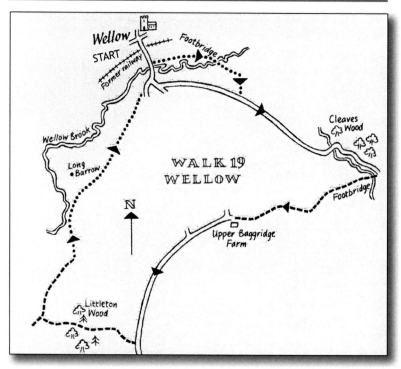

Turn left and follow the lane towards Norton St Philip for about a mile, past Norton Lane Farm, down and over a bridge which crosses Norton Brook, a tributary of Wellow Brook, then through woods.

Look out for a gap on the right leading to a footbridge across the stream – not the first metal-built one you spot but the mostly wooden one just beyond. Cross here and follow the stony track for some distance uphill. The way levels out as you reach the buildings of Baggridge Farm on the summit of **BAGGRIDGE HILL** and its many outbuildings, now neatly refurbished as separate dwellings.

From Upper Baggridge follow the ridge-top lane, past Grange Cottage, for almost a mile in a south-westerly direction until you reach a house at the edge of a wood. Turn right here along a wide track, signposted as a Byway, which descends the wooded hillside. This is a pretty, half-mile walk.

When you emerge from the wood there is a junction of ways: turn right by the signposted Public Bridleway with the hedgerow on your right. Head through a field crossing, then another. You will now be following a hedgerow on your left as you approach a ruined barn on your right. Down the valley you can see the church tower at Wellow looming over the village. Follow the hedge on your left and very soon drop down to reach a gate. Go through here and follow the hedgebank on your right to reach a further gate.

Go through and follow the rising path to reach a stile on the left, 50 yards or so below the top corrner. Climb over the stile and follow the hedgebank on your right until you reach a stile signposted to **STONEY LITTLETON LONG BARROW** (SLLB). This is a detour well worth the extra effort. Follow the hedge on your right until you reach a similarly signposted stile; cross here to reach the Barrow in its fenced enclosure.

Retrace your steps to the first SLLB signposted stile, cross over and turn left to reach the field gate. Go through here to follow a hedge on your right, continue across an open field, then gradually descend by way of an enclosed track to reach the lane where you bear left towards Wellow Brook. Now retrace your steps to your starting point in **WELLOW**.

Wellow footbridge and ford

BY THE WAY...

Wellow is a spacious and attractive village situated on a south-facing slope at between two and three hundred feet, its main street parallelled by the course of the former Cam Valley branch railway. The Fox and Badger pub, at the corner of Station Road, is recommended.

The pride of the village is its handsome church which stands in a commanding position at its northern edge. The building dates back to the late fourteenth-century, a comparatively late date for the origin of the village churches visited on the walks in this book. Wellow, in fact, is one of the very few villages in the area not mentioned in Domesday Book.

St Julian's Church displays an unusual consistency in its architecture – this in place of the jumble of periods and styles to which one is accustomed in village churches. The chancel was, in fact, rebuilt in 1890 but is a sympathetic restoration. The clerestory windows throw ample light onto an uncluttered interior. The intricate carving of the rood screen and the colourful sculptures in the Hungerford chapel provide a striking contrast to the plain grey stone of the main structure.

Baggridge: From this high and windy ridge there is a fine view in all directions: east and south beyond Norton St Philip towards Salisbury Plain, Cley Hill and the woods of Longleat. Up the valley to the west it is possible to see the pyramidal spoil heaps, now quite overgrown, and some of the villages associated with the long abandoned Somerset Coalfield. (For a concise account and a series of guided walks of this interesting area see *Colliers Way* by Peter Collier: Ex Libris Press, 1998).

Stoney Littleton Long Barrow: An explanatory panel offers some information about this well preserved monument. Do walk round to the entrance where you will find the door jambs (one of which displays a splendid ammonite cast) supporting a huge lintel where you can gain access to three pairs of burial chambers on either side of a central gallery, all dating from 5,000 years ago! It is quite possible to penetrate the farthest recesses of the tomb, some fifty feet from the entrance, and to inspect its fine construction, though you will have to crouch to do so.

*Stoney Littleton long barrow: from the outside looking in (left)
and from the inside looking out (right)*

20 WESTWOOD

via Stowford, Farleigh Castle and Iford

Distance:	4 miles
Maps:	Explorers 155, 156
	Landrangers 172, 173
Map Reference:	813590
Refreshment en route:	The New Inn at Westwood, the Hungerford Arms near Farleigh Castle. There are also tea rooms at Stowford.

THE WALK: Although an easy, short walk the route includes two manor houses, a beautiful parish church, a fifteenth century mill and a fourteenth century castle, a lost medieval village, as well as a beautiful stretch of the River Frome. This really is a surprisingly lovely short ramble and, although the last in this book, should not be missed.

DIRECTIONS

Opposite Westwood Manor there is a National Trust car park; this makes a convenient starting point for the walk. Look for the Public Footpath signpost and stile just beyond the car park. Cross the stile here and follow the direction indicated by the sign towards Stowford, i.e. straight across the field towards the clump of willows which surrounds a small pond. Continue into the next field.

Carry on in the same direction, straight ahead, until you reach a stile in the hedgerow. Again, in the next field, walk ahead to reach the crossing in the hedge. Now follow the beaten path, slightly downhill and veering gradually towards the right, then forking left. As the way levels out it becomes a more obvious track. Simply walk on towards the group of old stone buildings

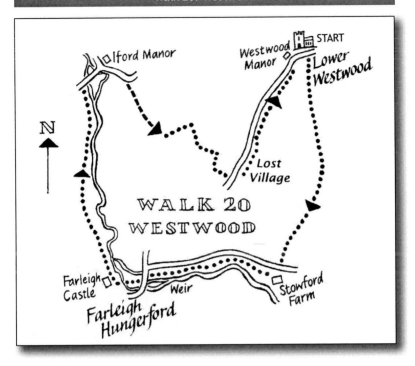

near the road; these are all in the vicinity of Stowford Farm.

Cross the road with care and enter the driveway into **STOWFORD** Farm and bear right. A permissive footpath follows the riverside meadow from Stowford towards the bridge at Farleigh Hungerford.

The permissive footpath traverses the riverside meadow. In the third field you will encounter the diving boards (now dismantled, thanks to Health and Safety!) belonging to the **Farleigh Hungerford Swimming Club** (For an interesting account of this venerable institution see Roger Deakin's book, *Waterlog*, Vintage, 2000). In the final field you head towards a stile in the far boundary to meet the road. Bear left to cross the bridges: one across the river proper; a second across a former mill leat.

This collection of buildings and those further uphill, including the church and pub the Hungerford Arms, comprise the small village of **Farleigh Hungerford**.

After the first bridge you can avoid the road up to the castle entrance by turning right before the pillar box and following the lane across the river to reach a point just below the ramparts of **FARLEIGH CASTLE**. You can bear left here and climb up to the castle entrance – this is also the way to go if you wish to seek refreshment at the Hungerford Arms, a pub which is located not far beyond the castle's entrance.

To continue the walk: follow the track below the castle walls and look out for the Footpath sign on the right which directs you across a plank bridge toward a kissing gate. Once through here you bear right to follow the river bank through several fields until you reach the lane at Iford. This is a wonderful stretch, but remember to look back towards the castle and the tower of Farleigh Hungerford church.

There is a second weir at Iford which once controlled the flow of a mill stream that powered the former Iford Mill. The iron sluice gates can be seen at the head of the mill stream. These have recently been joined by a small water turbine housed in the shed-like structure.

Turn right at the lane past the former mill and over the bridge to **IFORD Manor** (for description see Walk 1).

From Iford Manor turn right up the hill. Turn off onto the signposted bridleway, the entrance to which you will find a little way uphill on your right. This shady track climbs gently above the valley of the River Frome and offers some lovely views through gaps in the hedge.

The track eventually meets a stream and continues on the far side. Your route, however, requires you to cross the stream and then the kissing gate immediately on your left to enter a field. Now follow the left-hand boundary. Ignore the track which bears off to the left beside the sewerage works but keep to the beaten path between the fence and the field edge. Soon you turn through ninety degrees to the right, climb a little, turn to the left, then right once more, but always with the hedgerow on your left.

Eventually you reach a narrow, hedged track in the top corner of the last field; take this to reach the lane which connects Farleigh Hungerford with Westwood, but first look back towards the village of Westwood situated on the hill-top to the north, and down the valley of the River Frome toward Monkton Combe and the mushroom-like water tower on Bathampton Down.

Cross the lane and enter the field opposite by a stile.

This field, and the one on the far side of the lane, constitutes the site of the lost medieval village of Rowley. It is well worth entering this field to step across its hummocky surface. Somewhere towards the field's centre is a long hollowed-out stretch which it is tempting to believe was the village main street.

There is an exit from this field in the far left corner (facing towards Westwood). From here you have the choice either of returning to Westwood along the lane, which is generally very quiet (but mud-free), or negotiating the field path which runs parallel to the lane and just inside the hedgerow.

If you choose the green way, then climb over the stile to enter the next field on the right and follow the hedge toward **WESTWOOD** Church. You can continue in this direction all the way back to the stile at which you began this walk, close to the little car park opposite the entrance to Westwood Manor.

BY THE WAY ...

Westwood Manor and church make a fine group of ancient buildings on the edge of the village. The Manor belongs to the National Trust, has limited opening hours but is strongly recommended. It is difficult to do justice to the Manor and church in a few lines, particularly as there are excellent guide books available on both.

Westwood Manor is a diminutive building, in comparison to Great Chalfield or South Wraxall, and has portions dating from c. 1400, the late fifteenth-century and 1610. It was the rich clothier, Thomas Horton, commemorated in Holy Trinity Church in Bradford on Avon, who lived here and extended the house in the early 1600s. A fifteenth-century stone barn is sited to the east of the Manor whilst the church of St Mary is very close, being just to the south. The main feature of the church is its elaborate Somerset-type tower. The manor, especially, will repay a visit, when you may enjoy a guided tour.

Farleigh Castle

Stowford Mill, according to Wiltshire historian Kenneth Rogers, was leased by one William Sewey, clothman, in 1458, from Keynsham Abbey, so it may have been used as a fulling mill from that date. Its most prosperous time was the fifteenth century when the present house was built. Stowford was used as a centre for the production of wool and cloth for four centuries; in the mid-nineteenth-century it became a corn mill.

An old mill stood on the island between the two waterways and was the last country mill in the vicinity to close down; a fulling mill was recorded here in 1548 and was in action until 1910.

Farleigh Castle is open to the public, at a price, and is maintained by English Heritage. A leaflet is obtainable, from which the following sketch is largely culled. The original castle dates from the 1370s and was built by Sir Thomas Hungerford, a Wiltshire squire who was Speaker of the House of Commons in 1377. He died in 1398 and is buried in an enormous tomb chest in the chapel within the castle. His son, Sir Walter Hungerford, also a Speaker in the House, extended the castle by adding an outer court to enclose the former parish church and built the new church of St Leonard up the hill. Farleigh twice fell out of the possession of the Hungerfords and was twice repossessed. In the Civil War, the heir to Farleigh was commander of the Parliamentary forces in Wiltshire, and defeated his Royalist half-brother who had formerly occupied the castle. A later Hungerford, known as 'The Spendthrift', sold Farleigh in 1686, and it passed through various hands until placed under the guardianship of the Ministry of Works in 1919.

More books on Wiltshire and Somerset from Ex Libris Press ~

CURIOUS WILTSHIRE by Mary Delorme
Water Meadows, White Horses, Sarsen Stones, Dew Ponds, Blind Houses &
Tithe Barns. *ISBN 1 903341 09 4; Sixth reprint 2011; 160 pages; £7.95*

THE DAY RETURNS by John Chandler.
The perfect dipping-into book for all lovers of Wiltshire
ISBN 0 948578 95 5; 1998; 256 pages; £9.95

EXPLORING HISTORIC WILTSHIRE Volume 1: North by Ken Watts
Featuring six of the finest landscapes of rural north Wiltshire
ISBN 0 948578 92 0; Reprinted 2008; 176 pages; £7.95

THE GEOLOGY OF SOMERSET by Peter Hardy
ISBN 0 948578 42 4; Second reprint 2011; 224 pages; £9.95

GROWING UP IN WINSLEY: Marilyn's Story by Marilyn Maundrell
ISBN 978190664188 7; 72 pages; £4.95

HOSTS OF GHOSTS: Curious Happenings in West Wiltshire
by Margaret Dobson & Simone Brightstein.
ISBN 1 903341 29 9; 2005; 160 pages; £6.95

THE MARLBOROUGH DOWNS by Ken Watts
ISBN 1 903341 15 9; New edition 2003; 192 pages; £9.95

PRIVILEGED: A Freshford Boyhood by Michael Lintern
ISBN 978 1 906641 87 0; 94 pages; £5.95

Books on Bradford on Avon ~

BRADFORD ON AVON: PAST & PRESENT
by Harold Fassnidge
ISBN 978-1-903341-30-8; Revised and expanded edition 2007; 192 pages;
Price £9.95

BRADFORD VOICES: *Life in Bradford on Avon 1900-2010*
by Margaret Dobson
ISBN 978-906641-36-8; New & enlarged edition, 2011; 320 pages; Price £11.95

BRADFORD ON AVON'S SCHOOLS: *The Story of Education in a small Wiltshire
town* by Keith Berry
ISBN 0-948578-96-3; 240 pages; Price £8.95

BRADFORD ON AVON'S PUBS AND BREWERIES
by Jack Mock
ISBN 978-1-906641-40-5; 2012; 96 pages; Price £5.95

BRYLCREEM AND BROKEN BISCUITS by Stephanie Laslett
ISBN 978-1-906641-57-3; 112 pages; £6.95

All the above titles are available via our website, post-free, using Paypal
www.ex-librisbooks.co.uk